Ibstock Lives

Edited by Jeanne Carswell

The production of this book would not have been possible without financial assistance from the following:

Ibstock Parish Council

David Wilson Homes Ltd

Leicestershire and South Derbyshire Rural Initiatives Fund

Leicestershire County Council Museums, Arts and Records Service

North West Leicestershire Arts Council

Ibstock Building Products Ltd.

The Springboard Centre (Coalville) Ltd.

Thanks also go to:

Ibstock Historical Society

Staff at Leicestershire Libraries, Ibstock Branch: Jean and Dena

Garryson Ltd

Typists: Vivien Parry, Linda Green and Steven Peace

Help with typesetting: Steve Duckworth

Proof reading: Lawrence Grady

The judges who prefer to remain anonymous

The people who lent the photographs: Frances Davies, Jean Lines, Jean Middleton, Pat Mee, Harold Talbott, Jim Satchwell, Iliffe Webster, Syd and Florrie Wallace.

ISBN 1 872479 15 4

Printed by The Alden Press Oxford

FOREWORD

IBSTOCK LIVES is the result of a writing competition instigated by Ibstock Parish Council to commemorate its centenary year. People were invited to write or tape-record their personal memories of their village. Over forty entries were received and the judges felt that the standard was extremely high. It was very difficult to choose winners and in the end three pieces were chosen as joint first prize winners. It was felt that these best represented the warmth of feeling that Ibstockians had, and still have, for their village. The judges also highly commended six other entries. The memories cover the period from the 1890s to the 1960s. Many of the competitors take the reader for the same walk along High Street. These are all included as they serve, in some way, to illustrate how things have changed over the years.

The book starts with the three prize winners, followed by the highly commended entries. Then there is a section devoted mainly to childhood, which was the favoured choice of most of the competitors. The part that war played in some people's lives comes next, followed by a section dealing with how leisure time was spent and a miscellany of reminiscences. At the end is a fanciful account of an early meeting of the local council which, I am assured, bears no resemblance to what happens in meetings today.

For me it was a great pleasure to be involved in the competition, to be given the opportunity to have a glimpse of how Ibstock used to be and to meet past and present-day villagers. Every entry is represented in this book and I hope that readers will enjoy reading them as much as I did.

Jeanne Carswell

Parish Councils - A Brief History

Parish Councils in England date from 1894. The Local Government Act of 1894 introduced the Parish Meeting and the Parish Council as institutions to have civil origin and status. The Act transferred the civil functions of older authorities to the new Parish Councils.

Up to 1894, the leaders of villages had been the squire, the parson or the schoolmaster. They were regarded as the educated people of the villages and the parish vestries took advice from them. From November 1894 the churchwardens ceased to be the parish overseers and the legal interests of property etc. were vested from the Church to the new parish councils.

Ibstock Parish Council of ten members was formed from a poll taken in December 1894. The Council first met in 1895 and the minute books go back to that year.

A Burial Board was formed in 1881, after the donation, by T T Paget MP, of the land in Peggs Lane (Pretoria Road). That Board was transferred to the Parish Council in 1901. The Council adopted street lighting powers in 1900.

Ibstock Parish Council has had five clerks:

Francis Holmes	1895 - 1938
Harry Lawrence	1938 - 1970
Bill Bourne	1970 - 1980
Ron Bartlett	1981 - 1988
David Price	1989 -

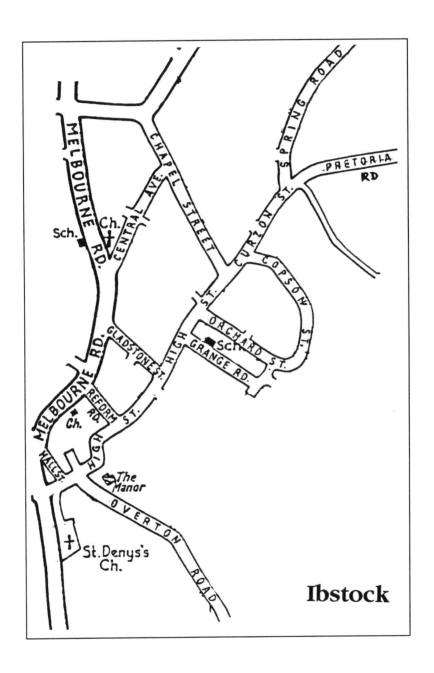

Ibstock

The First Prize Winners

Jeanette Dexter - submitted by Iliffe Webster, Ibstock

Jean Lines, Ibstock

Pat Mee, Coalville

Highly Commended

Frances Davies, Ibstock

Frank Gregory, Bagworth

Florence Bradley, Ibstock

D Middleton, Ibstock

S Wallace, Ibstock

George Moore, Ibstock

Ibstock Lives by Paula Gretton

Our village of Ibstock is very old,
Over a thousand years or more.
There's many a story could be told,
Of people rich and poor.
There's a mention in the Domesday Book,
Of Ibba and his stockade,
But further back, if you care to look,
You'll find relics from a Roman brigade.

The Church was the old village centre,
Many people have worshipped here.
There was a Rector who became a King's mentor
Who thought he had nothing to fear.
As Canterbury's Archbishop he angered the King,
Not knowing what was at stake,
When once the King his praises did sing.
To lose his life was to be his fate.

As we come back along the years,
More famous names come to mind.
There have been some, so don't you jeer,
Let's see who else we might find.
Alderman Jacques was a man of great worth,
Who gave his great name to a street,
And Bernard Newman, this is the place of his birth,
You can sit by his name on a seat.

Do you remember these things of the past?
Queuing up for the threepenny rush,
Or sucking gobstoppers and making them last.
Is that an Indian hiding in that bush?
The famous Red Garries marching down the street,
With uniforms sparkling and bright.
The Salvation Army at the Scout Hut did meet
For pea suppers and sing-a-long nights.

Those were the days, people didn't go very far.
In the village every need could be met.
Dr Meldrum's one of the few with a car
And the cakes at Mee's bakery, who could forget?
Perhaps these words have stirred up your thoughts
For by children and grown-ups as well,
Your memories are such that they'll always be sought.
You must have some tales to tell!

This winning contribution is taken from a tape-recording made with Mrs Jeanette Dexter when she was 97 years old. Mrs Dexter had worked as a nurse and she died in 1990, in the Kathleen Rutland Home for the Blind, just a few weeks short of her hundredth birthday. The tape was submitted by her nephew, Iliffe Webster.

I was born in 1890 in the jitty off High Street. My father had a house built next to the Star on the corner of Orchard Street. He had it as a boot shop one side and a small tobacco shop on the other and that's where I was brought up. I was five when we went to live there. My brother Haydn and my sister Hilda were born in the new house. The Post Office was next to it - the very old Post Office - Mr Badcock kept that. There were one or two shops and some houses just beyond until you came to Grange Road where the National School was. The infants school was in Grange Road. The headmistress there in my time was Miss Meek. We used to arrive there in the morning with our sandwiches tied up with string. She would collect them and we ate those at lunch hour. Early on we just went to school in the morning, later on we stayed all day. There was the Church of England school in the village and the rector, Mr Ford, used to come to the school. I remember that he had a long black beard, right down to his chest. He was quite a nice old man.

Coming up Grange Road to the left was the National School and then a few more shops beyond that. There was Bonser's, a hardware shop. They had a very nice house and a very nice shop. Then there were two little cottages and a lane, then a butcher's and another boot shop. Next there was a very old place which was used by a very old man. I think he owned the pub on the other side of the road. On the left hand side were shops and a big house. It is now used as the Legion House. Mr Jacques lived there - he owned the quarry at Heather (one of the big pots in the village). He always went about dressed in a tail coat. Then there were one or two ordinary shops - a little grocer's and a greengrocer's, a butcher's which is still a butcher's shop - Newman's. Next was Dr Thomas's surgery. He had an assistant, Dr Agnew who married Dr Thomas's daughter. I can remember them getting married. For the wedding, all the streets were lined with flags.

Going round Manton's corner, you came to some grounds which belonged to the Manor House. After that was the Church which is very old. Everybody used to go to the church, but there were just a few non-conformists who were considered to be nobody in those days. You didn't know them. Next to that was a huge house which belonged to the Church. I never went inside but my mother and her sister did and

1

Mother said that they were terrified of it as it was so big. The Wilemans used to live in the White House and we thought that was very posh. I should imagine that it was once a coaching house as there were stables at the back.

Years ago the Pagets lived in the Manor House and they are buried in the churchyard in great big tombs. The Pagets eventually left Ibstock and went to live at Roehampton. They named their house Ibstock Place. Then we come to Manton's Corner again. Miss Hind, a maiden lady, lived where the day nursery is now. As far as I know, she lived alone and she always reminded us of Queen Victoria. She owned houses in Pretoria Road and used to go through the village to collect the rents in a pony and trap. There was a coachman on the front and we used to bow to her as she went through. There was a big grocery shop - Thirlby's. That was THE place to shop in Ibstock. I used to go there on Saturday mornings and he used to always say, "I'm glad you've come. I can have one of those curls now, can't I?"

On the other side of the road where the Health Centre now is, used to be Pickworths. My mother worked there. She was said to have been a Court dressmaker and she used to do all the dresses for the big pots there. Then you came to Deacon's Lane with a pub on the corner - the Whimsey - then the Bankhouse. At the side was Newman's the farmers. Their house stood quite a long way back with a yard at the back where they had the cattle. Then there was Richardson's - they had dresses, haberdashery and everything. It was a lovely shop. It is Megan's now. Next to that was a cottage where you had to go up some steps. A miserable old woman lived there and we used to have to take her a dinner on a Sunday. It was almost a Christian act because she lived by herself but she was a miserable old whatsaname and was never grateful. We used to take her lovely dinners that my mother used to put up for her.

Then there was Preston's, butchers, and next a beer-off which was the other side of the jitty to the house where I was born. Then there was Harratt's house - more 'people of the village'. They were coffin makers and did everything in the wood line. It was a trade that had been going for years. They were big Church people. Beyond them was a jeweller's. I remember their housekeeper who was a snuff taker. She used to come to our tobacco shop, always on a Sunday morning, to buy snuff. My mother refused to sell it to her but she used to stand there pleading with Mother until she sold it to her. Then there was another butcher's shop, two or three houses which stood back and had cobbled yards and a shop at the corner of Chapel Street.

Saturday was the busiest day in the High Street because it was market day when the farmers came into the village. I don't think we had a market as such. There would be just a few stalls with the farmers' cheese and butter.

I can remember the first car that came into Ibstock. It came along the High Street and there was a man with a red flag to warn us of the danger. It was possibly the first car in the district and they were probably bringing it along the High Street just to let everyone know. It was a novelty to see a car being driven without a horse at the front. There were only horses and traps then and the streets were all cobbled - awful to walk on. Grange Road used to be all fields and that is where the brook was. The brook went from the colliery to Locker's Lane. We used to go to the brook and then we would have a good hiding for getting wet. We used to walk across the fields to Battram. The only way of getting anywhere was across the fields.

Mr Cramp, the violin maker, was my grandfather. He played the double bass, Uncle John played the the cello and both my father and Uncle Enoch played the violin. My grandfather made double basses and my father made several cellos. They used to go out playing everywhere. The last cello my father made was given by my mother to a young man from the school who was learning the cello but couldn't afford to buy one. The Cramps were a very musical family. My father belonged to an orchestra and I think Uncle Enoch did too. Music was all my father thought about. When I was a girl, I was put to learn the piano. The little tobacco shop was our parlour and the piano was in there. When I was having lessons the children used to come and peer through the window and they wanted to know why I wasn't going out. I wanted to get out to play and therefore I didn't practise. The teacher told my father that it wasn't a bit of good him paying money out for me to learn because I wouldn't practise. And I wouldn't. I've never touched a piano from that day. It was a great disappointment to my father. He wanted one of us to play the piano and the others to play the cello and none of us did. We just tinkled. Hilda tinkled on the piano and my brother could play the violin a bit but none of us took it seriously.

My father played the violin and Mr Arnott from the farm who played the cello used to come every weekend for musical evenings. The Sunday School Anniversary, in those days, was a musical event. There was always an orchestra and everybody went. From the first Sunday in May until September, my father was out every Sunday playing for some event. We used to go out in a horse brake for the Sunday School treat to a field next to a pub at the edge of Coalville. We used to go there and have a tea and play games. I can remember that we could pick bilberries in the grounds there. It took about half an hour to get to Coalville from Ibstock by brake and the fare was threepence when they first started the service. Another place I liked to go to was Bardon Hill. It was a very high spot and we could go there for a picnic. If you went to Leicester past the Flying Horse at Markfield, the bluebell woods were a picture. They are all gone now. There has been a lot of building.

We used to have hoops to bowl along and we played marbles in the street. Another thing we were very fond of was tying door knockers together. We used to knock the doors and run away. People would come to answer the doors and then wonder why they couldn't open them.

There was some awful poverty in Ibstock. Near the cemetery was a row of houses in Meadow Road. The people there had no money and they were very dirty. I think the houses belonged to the colliery and the men worked at the colliery. I've heard

Mother say that the men would go to the Ram public house on Friday nights and spend all their money on drinking so that when they got home they hadn't got a penny left for their families. Mrs Palmer who ran the Ram was a lovely woman. She kept the place very clean and she wouldn't have swearing. At the back of the Ram was the cricket field where we used to have the Wakes. The fair used to come on a Friday and set up. Then we had Saturday, Monday and Tuesday - they didn't operate on a Sunday. That was the highlight of the year. There was the merry-go-round with the horses going up and down, great big swingboats and coconut shies. My father always used to go and win us a coconut. That was a great event.

William Cramp Jnr and his Second Wife, Fanny Cramp

The second winning entry comes from Jean Lines. Jean was born in 1936, has lived in Ibstock all her life and is an active member of the local Church. She works in Ibstock Library and, in her spare time, pursues her hobby of needlecraft.

Happy memories spent in Ibstock (before T.V.) in the days of whip and top, hopscotch, skipping and hoop and stick. What a life - no money but we were happy and contented with what we had, even coming home from school was an adventure or, looking back, an assault course. Going to school was no problem, as we lived up Pretoria Road (Common Hill). Straight to school and no messing was the order of the day. After school we often went home the scenic route, from the junior school down the jitty, down Orchard Street, round the black path (little did I know that later in life I would live on the black path), up Copson Street, along Curzon Street. Call at Gran Riley's for a hot potato in newspaper (to eat going along), walk along everybody's front wall and jump the gates, hoping you didn't get caught. On to the brook and the rails, where we would spend ten minutes or so tippling over, then to the gas works opposite - this had a high wall where we could practise hand stands, up to the cemetery wall, again to do hand stands. Through the fields at the side of the cemetery, round the back of the houses picking flowers as we went, climb some buildings left because of the war, look for newts down the dug out well, climb two tree trunks at the bottom of the brickyard and then I was home. Mam would say, "Where have you been?" I'd just say, "Coming."

As children we always had something to look forward to, either through school, Sunday School or with our own friends and family. We would look forward to the Good Friday concert and practise in chapel for weeks before the event. It always got a full chapel, the children would do their bit first, usually a play. Mrs George Wilson would get us together and give us our parts and we would learn them religiously and Mrs Gwen Mugglestone would accompany the singing on the piano. We always had more children than parts but everyone got in somehow. The adults would do a grown-up play after, which on Good Friday we would be allowed to watch.

The next event would be the Sunday School Anniversary (the Sermons). Again, this called for weeks of practice and generated lots of excitement as we prepared for the big day. Curzon Street Methodist Sermons were always the third Sunday in May. So on the first and second Sunday we went to the Wesleyan and Wes Reform Chapel to see if their platforms were higher than ours (ha ha). If given a choice, I'm sure us children would have gone to where the platforms were the highest.

After the Sermons, we had the Sunday School outing. Ours was always to Abbey Park but it seemed miles away. Probably three bus loads would go and we would spend most of the time shouting at the driver to catch the bus in front - pass him, pass him - it was deafening. The drivers must have been very special because they always took part and the ride, I think, was the most exciting part of the day.

The Working Men's Club took us on an outing once a year. This time we had bottles of pop and crisps - free. Parents travelled on a separate bus, my travelling time was spent wondering if I would ever see them again. We usually went to Wicksteed Park and it seemed ages to get there.

Besides events from school and Sunday School, we had our own interests. I remember my parents selling my doll's pram and the money from this went towards buying me a bike but I wanted a basket on the front so I had to work for it. I did everybody's shopping and saved one penny at a time. I collected jam jars and tea coupons (and priced the basket every other week). The big day came - eleven shillings and sixpence in a box. I called at Fowkes' shop in Chapel Street where this lovely old lady all dressed in black looked at me. She knew what I wanted. I'd been in so many times she said, "You look as if you've raided your money box, just give me eleven shillings." I will never forget that kindness.

I remember Dad telling us stories about when he was young and we realised his childhood was very different to our own. One particular story will always remain with me. We didn't know Grandma Ball, my dad's family had split up before Mam and Dad married but we had seen photos of her. We knew she taught music and we knew Grandad liked a drink and a fight. We also knew that Grandma Ball had run away but nobody knew where.

Jean Lines' Grandma Ball

During the Summer holidays our parents took us on holiday. We were told we were going to Llandudno. We stayed in a terraced house with a lady we called Aunty Lizzie and a man called Uncle Bill. They were really lovely people and Aunty Lizzie played the piano. I remember lying in bed listening to her playing, it was wonderful and next morning I asked what certain pieces were called and she talked to me a lot. I became very fond of her. One morning I realised that a photograph she had was the same as one we had at home and I said so and then, suddenly, I knew that this lovely lady, who taught music and played so beautifully, was my grandma. It caused a bit of a panic and I was asked to keep it a secret (it doesn't matter now). I was so proud to know my grandma. However, when we went back to school we had to write about our holidays. Mine was spent in Llandudno or so I thought. I described the journey and talked about fishing and surroundings etc and the teacher had me in front of the class. I hadn't been to Llandudno at all, I'd been to Highley in Shropshire. My grandma's hiding place and my dad's big secret was all revealed.

As I grew up I kept our secret because it could have been quite dangerous for my gran to return to Ibstock. After the death of my grandad (Big Sam) my gran came back and was married by special licence at Coalville Register Office (were the good old days so good?).

As a child I was always willing to do errands on my bike and one of my favourite errands was to take my dad's pick blade to be sharpened at the blacksmith's. This was up Harratt's yard (now Harratt's Close). What a man, even as a child I was aware of his strength and I remember he never spoke, he just worked away, sweating profusely. I used to go up the yard hoping that there would be a horse there to be shod. I hated the smell when he put the new shoe on but I loved to watch him work. I always waited for my dad's pick blade and the only time he spoke was to tell me to stand back when he was making the sparks fly. I used to stand in the way on purpose just to make him speak.

I also liked to fetch the carbide, for my dad's pit lamp, from Bott's shop or Randall's. These shops were ironmongers and were in the High Street. I remember Mr Bott was always singing! Well, no words but a pleasant sound. I can smell these shops now, they had their own pungent odour. If it was a wet day I used to drop carbide in a puddle just to see it fizz up.

Our pleasures in life cost nothing really, we were so happy and pleased with what we had - the love of two wonderful parents.

This winning entry came from Pat Mee, who was born into the Adcock family which is mentioned more than once in this book. After working for various local companies, Pat became a mature student and now teaches at Hugglescote Primary School.

School days are the happiest days of your life - so they say! Well, they must be because at fifty-five I'm still at school.

My first school days were spent at the infants school in Grange Road. My grandma got me off to school as Mum worked at the factory on Melbourne Road, making chin straps for the war effort.

The day would begin with my mum waking me up, taking me through the connecting door from our living room, through the shop into their living room, up the stairs and into Grandma's warm bed. I snuggled up to Grandma until it was time to get up.

Grandad got up first to make the fire by emptying the ashes, chopping the wood folding the paper and lighting the fire. Grandma would get up and put the kettle of water on to the open fire to boil. She set the table for breakfast with new crusty bread from Mee's bakery, hard margarine and home-made blackberry jam. I would make the toast but as I held the thick round of bread over the fire, on the wire toasting fork, I would often burn my legs until they looked like a patchwork quilt.

Alan Ball would call for me to go to school and sometimes Alan Pettitt or Audrey Preston. It just depended if we had fallen out or not the day before.

The infant school seemed huge but only consisted of four classrooms. Mrs Cooper was my first teacher, she was so kind and considerate. She would put our initials at the bottom of our milk beakers, the girls in pink and the boys in blue. Mary Smith and Mary Storer presented her with a problem but one had a picture of a house on it and the other had M.S. The room was bright with well used pictures on the walls. The windows were high and we couldn't see out of them and, depending on where you sat, you were either roasted by the open fire or frozen at the back of the room.

Miss Holmes taught me how to knit, in fact she taught everyone how to knit - all at the same time .... in, round, cast off. When you 'got very good' you could knit a dishcloth and you didn't have to undo it, then you could take it home.

Mrs Bradford was the next teacher. She rode to school on a 'sit up and beg' bicycle. She had plaited hair which she would wind round into two coils at the side of her head. Her earrings were gorgeous and were envied by the girls in the class. We wrote on a small slate using a slate pencil and how she kept records of our progress I'll never know. Miss Lander was our headmistress and spoke with a soft but firm voice, unless she was reprimanding Gerald Hardington, Michael Vaughan or Selwyn Ottey.

Most of us would walk home for our dinner but I remember going to the hall on the other side of Grange Road for dinner sometimes.

Everywhere we went we had to carry our gas masks, even to school. Looking back, they could have been used when we visited the toilets across the playground! During the winter term these toilets were frequently frozen over and a visit to the them just to waste time in school never entered your head (well, only the toughest ones).

I was very sad to leave this school and go to the junior school on Melbourne Road. Mr Harratt was the headmaster, you could say master in those days, and I was terrified of the thought of a man teaching me.

My next four years at this school were very happy and 'Daddy' Harratt was brill! I was first taught by Miss Harratt and then a Miss Farmer who, looking back, must have suffered from hay-fever as she was constantly blowing her nose loudly and then putting her soggy wet pieces of 'rag' hankies to dry on the radiators. Miss Johnson taught the third year and Mr Lewis year four.

After school we would all rush home, crossing the Melbourne Road at the 'jitty'. There was no lollipop lady then but then there were no cars either. A visit to Allen's shop 'just to look' was the next port of call and then we would walk up to the black sheds in Harratt's yard to watch them mending the wheels for the horse and carts. There was always a blazing fire and a clanging banging noise as the metal rims were made to size.

We would only look at the sweets in Moreton's little shop, the one that jutted out from the Palace, as we never had enough coupons to get any, even if we had any money.

Tea was always ready for me. Ibstock provided everything we needed. Bread from Mee's bakehouse, often served by Ernie himself, after giving out the latest Billet news. Milk from Archie Crane who delivered every morning by horse and cart, slopping the milk out of the churns into a waiting jug, and jam made by your mum or grandma from the blackberries gathered from 'Grassy Lane'. We didn't have much but as we switched on the wireless to listen to Mrs Dale's Diary and how worried she was about him, the war seemed far away.

The shop door would open and Grandad would shout, "It's only me." He'd just walked back from his allotment at the bottom of Common Hill. Everyone had an allotment to 'dig for victory', as well as to provide vegetables in order to live. On Fridays he'd return from a day in Leicester. He went there to fetch sheet music or records for people who lived in Ibstock. They'd bring in their order during the week and collect it on a Friday night or Saturday morning.

One Friday night ritual was a bath, in the zinc bath in front of the fire. Everyone used the same water and the youngest member of the family went in first. We often had a visitor at the door who would just stand talking while you sat in the bath with the water getting cold! Drying yourself was done in double quick time. No central heating then, only a coal fire. It was a dose of syrup of figs next, just to make sure you were 'regular' and frizzled cheese for supper. If it was a cold night you would get warmth from an oven shelf, wrapped up in a blanket, instead of a water bottle in your bed.

Breakfast would sometimes consist of a slice of bacon, cut from the flitch hanging on the wall, especially Sunday breakfasts, and mushrooms picked from the fields the night before.

I hated the nights when the lavatories were emptied. Two men would carry the open lavatory pans down the entry and then tip them into the cart standing in the road. The smell was terrible. We were always told to be in bed before the ten o'clock horses came and I can see why now! Visiting the loo at night was quite a trauma. I needed someone to stand on the garden path to wait for me while I trekked to the bottom of the garden. There was no soft, coloured tissue paper then only sheets of newspaper carefully cut into squares, threaded with string and hung onto a nail. Once we tried some purple tissue paper that Cyril Greasley had his apples wrapped in. It was so soft, we thought it was great until we found that if left a purple stain in a peculiar place.

If I had any spare money I'd go to the threepenny rush at the Palace. I could get money if Mr Restall was buying rose hips that week and I'd had a good day's picking down Locker's Lane. The front row of the pictures was always very popular, that is until the film began, then it would gradually empty. Some would crawl underneath the seats so as to sit on the red plush ones half-way back and some of us got to the doubles on the back row. The boys just went to the gents, outside, never to return. They decided that the cricket or football game in the Ram field was more entertaining than the Lone Ranger. Besides Mr Ball often stopped the film to shout, "If anyone else laughs they will go out." (That was when a Laurel and Hardy film was on!!)

Life seemed great and there were always lots of games to play, such as marbles in the gutter, pestering Georgie Cornwall or trying to get Billy Riley to swallow the tacks that he put in his mouth while he mended the shoes.

Sometimes, we'd get some warm bread from Mee's shop and one penny's worth of chips from Mrs Moreton's and sit on the wall between the bakehouse and my grandparents' shop, just watching the world go slowly by.

There'd be the Church parade, the Band of Hope on a Saturday night, Brownies with Gertrude Buckingham, a game of rounders in Copson Street (undisturbed by traffic and 'snobs'.

Looking back, those schooldays seemed to be so happy but then, perhaps, we only remember the happy times.

Childhood Memories by Florence Bradley

I began my life in Battram Lane, Ellistown on the 11 April 1908. I was there for twelve months, then my parents brought me to 27 Grange Road, Ibstock. My grandma came to live with us and she made a great fuss of me. My earliest recollection is of my grandma lifting me on to a chair, to watch her making jam tarts. She even let me cut some out, I loved that. When I was four years old, I remember she took me to Heather Station to collect a pushchair. It was then I saw my first train. I ran, screaming, I thought it was a monster. Everyone ran after me, I was terrified. Grandma consoled me until I was calm.

I started school when I was five years old. I was very lucky that the school was in Grange Road, so I did not have far to go. In my class we had trays of sand in which we had to draw a spade, the kind that children use at the seaside. We also had cardboard rings and we had to wind coloured wool round them, they made lovely rainbow rings. In the infant class there was a rocking horse and I longed to have a ride on it but I never did. I never forgot it.

I do not remember much about the next class that I went in but I must have done something special because the teacher gave me a lovely book called 'Cinderella'. I was so excited with it that I ran out of school and my dad was just going by the school gates. He was very black because he was coming from the pit and there were no baths then. I showed him my book and I am sure that he was pleased with me.

A few months after that my grandma passed away. I do not remember crying but I am sure that I must have done. I can remember my mam lifting me up to see Grandma as she lay in bed and I thought she was asleep because she looked so peaceful. They did not take the dead away when I was a child, the relatives had to keep them at home until the funeral.

As I grew older I used to wander down to the fields with the other children and, in the Spring, we made daisy chains and put them around our heads, pretending that we were princesses. The fields were only two minutes walk away from our house. We had a recreation ground, with swings, we called it the reccy. We spent lots of happy hours there. We would jump the brook (I forgot to mention there was a brook at the bottom of the field) and we would see who could jump the widest part of the brook. There was many a one fell in!! When we had had enough of that, we would go picking violets from under the hedge along the top of the field.

In the Summer we used to play lots of games, such as hide and seek, skipping (I loved that), whip and top, marbles and lots more.

When Autumn came, we children would get together and go blackberrying. We had such fun, we walked miles, never thinking about the walk back. I am afraid that we did not have many blackberries left by the time we got home. We would be hungry, so we ate most of them.

Winters were also great fun. We used to have a lot of snow when I was young an we built snow-houses and snowmen. I remember getting hot-aches (Mam calle them that). Mam would get me to put my hands in the boiler at the side of th fireplace, that would soon warm my hands. Of course, it was not boiling hot. always wanted to go out again but Mam used to say, "Don't come in crying again."

I used to love to see the lamplighter come down our road, to light the gas lamps.

As I grew older Mam found my sister and me a few tasks to do about the house such as washing-up and dusting. Then I had to start going on errands. I did no mind that as much, as long as I did not meet the cows, going to be milked. I wa scared to death of them (I still am).

I used to see a chimney sweep ride through the village, in a horse and trap, singin at the top of his voice, 'The Old Village Bells'. The men and boys used to whistle lot when I was young, you never hear them now. I wonder why!

When I went to the older school, at the top of our road, I felt really grown up. liked school and I seemed to get on well with everyone. When we came out o school, my friend and I used to sit on the edge of the pavement playing 'snobs'. W found five white stones, all the same size, to play with. There was one particula part that we dare not play on. It was opposite our school and we were told that i we sat there the old lady living there would throw a bucket of water over us. Th lady concerned always wore a sunbonnet and she was called Maria.

The First World War finished when I was ten years old. My dad joined the Ibstoc Silver Prize Band and when it was Parade Sunday, they would march all around th village. I was very proud of dad in his uniform and I told everyone near me, "That' my dad." He played the big bass instrument.

On Saturday afternoons, Dad would give my sister and me a penny to go to th Palace. We always went early but we still had to queue for ages before we coul get in. Then, when we did get in it was bedlam. It was better when the pictur started, as we settled down to watch the films. We booed the villain and cheere the hero and heroine. When I came out of the Palace, I can remember feelin flushed and excited. I wished I could be as beautiful as the heroine I had just bee watching. I noticed that the boys, who had been to the pictures, were acting lik cowboys. I believe that the films had a big influence on us children. I alway dreamed of being a big actress - but it was only a dream, I was soon back to reality

We were very poor and my parents had a struggle to bring us up. I remembe having a hole in the heel of my black stocking and I pulled it under my heel to hid it. If we had bread and cheese we could not have butter on our bread. On Saturda nights Mam filled a tin bath with hot water and put us in it one by one, me first as was the eldest. I suppose I was lucky as I had the clean water but I am afraid that used to cry because the soap used to get in my eyes. I had long hair and it made i much harder for Mam to rinse my hair properly. It could not have done it any harn though, as one of my neighbours said that it looked like ripe corn. I was very proud of my hair and I was always pestering mam to put it in rags to make curls like Mary Pickford, she was the 'World's Sweetheart'. I was beginning to get rather vain at that time and when someone told me that I would become beautiful if I went down to the fields early every morning to wash my face in the morning dew, I tried it for a while but soon got tired of getting up early and not becoming beautiful.

I remember the milkman coming round every morning in his horse and float. He had a large churn which had several measures - half a pint, one pint and one quart. I loved watching him measure the milk out. He did not come to our house as we could not afford milk at that time. If Mam had any coppers to spare, she would send me to Mr White's, just up the road from where we lived. He had a small holding and kept cows. I would go for a penny worth of milk. Then there was the rag and bone man, he would be shouting, "Rags, bones and rabbit skins." If we took anything like that to him he would give us a windmill. I used to think it would be easy to make one of those, just a stick with four sails made of coloured cardboard that were tacked on to it. They did not last very long.

I remember a horse and cart coming round the village with almost everything on it, even a large tin of paraffin. If anyone wanted any they brought a tin with them and the man put a tundish in to measure it out.

The night soil men came round every Friday night to empty the pans. The pans were situated in closets (that's what we called them), they were across a yard from us. It seemed such a long way away when you needed to use them.

We didn't have television and radio but we always found something to do in the Winter nights. Mam would start making a rag rug and when I was old enough she would let me help her. I liked to peg the rags in but I did not like cutting the rags because it hurt my fingers. Mam would cut a certain length to start me and I had to cut the others like that one. The peg was half of an ordinary clothes peg that had been sharpened. We had a paraffin lamp for lighting, that is when Mam could afford the paraffin. If not, we had a candle.

When I was about nine years old, Mam heard that we could get some margarine from the Maypole Shop in Coalville, if we could get there. Some of the older children in the row where I lived offered to go. I begged Mam to let me go. We were very short of food at the time and I suppose she thought that I would be alright with the other children. I thought that it was a big adventure. We walked to Coalville and arrived at the Maypole. I thought it was great. We had to queue for ages, it seemed like hours and it was so cold but it was well worth it when we finally made it to the shop. We bought margarine and we were allowed a jar of jam. While I was in Coalville I saw some men in light blue suits, some were on crutches. I was told that they had been wounded in the war and had been sent home. I can't remember the walk back from Coalville but I must have arrived home alright.

Every Sunday the 'okey' man would come round and, if we had a half-penny, we would buy a cornet and we would try to make it last a long time by biting off the bottom of the cornet and sucking the 'okey' from there. We called it 'okey' but really it's called ice-cream.

During the war I saw some pictures taken of some of the battles that took place; the one I remember the most was of the Battle of the Somme. I was told that we lost thousands of men, but it did not seem real to me. I suppose that's how it affects a child. We did not have many men killed who lived near to us or we might have been affected more.

I am going to take a walk now along the High Street and point out to you the shops that were there when I was about nine years old. I'll start from our church at the end of the village and the beautiful avenue that leads to it. In the Spring and Summer I have never seen a more beautiful avenue. I walk from there by the old stables (the church hall now) by Locker's Lane (this is now Overton Road), round the corner and I come to Mr Manton's shop. He was a painter and decorator and, I think, he must have done a bit of plumbing as he had a toilet on display in the shop window. Next came Crane's farmyard, then by two or three houses, then Mr Thirlby's grocery store and his house. Next came Mr Dunstan's house. He was the headmaster of our school, most of the children liked him, in fact, someone made a verse up about him:

Mr Dunstan's a nice old man,

He tries to teach you all he can,

Reading, writing and arithmetic,

But he never forgets to give you the stick,

He makes you dance

Out of England into France,

Out of France into Spain,

Over the hills and back again.

I come to a blacksmith's forge next, this belonged to Mr Mears, then Dr Agnew's house and surgery. Next to this was a drapery shop, kept by Miss Knight, then Mr Newman's butcher's shop, after that was Brown's boot and shoe shop. I can't remember who kept the next shop. The one next to this was a grocery shop owned by Mr Sharpe. He was a nice old gentleman with a beard.

Mr and Mrs Ottey kept the next shop. It was a greengrocery and I loved the smell in there. After that came the saddler's shop, where there were always leather belts hanging up in the window. Next came the barber's shop, I believe Mr Smith kept that. There was a driveway next leading now to the 'Motts' - home of Mr Jacques. I believe that he was a councillor. Across from the barber's shop was a jewellery shop, owned by someone called Moss. There was a yard next and I feel sure there was a cottage down there.

14

Next was another butcher's shop owned by a Mr Dunnicliffe. Then there was a boot and shoe shop, belonging to Mrs Eggington, also a small sweet shop owned by Mrs Eggington. Then came another butcher's shop, owned by Mr Fletcher. There was an opening leading to the fields and by the opening there were two small cottages. Then Mrs Bonsor's drapery shop. Mrs Bonsor had two lovely daughters and I remember that they were very kind to me when I went into the shop. I was told that the next building had been a butcher's shop. It had wire over the window and it looked dark and dreary. I always hurried by there. Next to that was a large house, I suppose that the school caretaker lived there. I am not sure about that. Our school was next door, at the top of Grange Road.

I cross over from there and come to Steele's shop. Mr Steele was a painter and decorator and used to have lovely wallpaper in the window. After that I pass by several houses and then come to Mr Wheartcroft's shop, it was a hardware shop and he sold almost everything. Next was a gents' shop owned by Mr Shuttleworth, then a yard with big doors on it. I can remember there being a Bazaar in there but I can only remember going in there once, so I don't know how long it was there. The newspaper shop was next, I was told it was the Post Office as well. I remember looking in the window and seeing a comic called 'Chips'. I could see Weary Willie

Cramp's Tobacconist and Boot Shop

15

and Tired Tim on the front page. Then next door was Cramp's shop, then the Star.

Across the top of Orchard Street was the chemist kept by Mr Simpson, at that time. I can remember a big blue bottle being in the window. Then came Mr Knifton's shop that was a barber's shop, then Mrs Rolleston's shop, she sold all kinds of material. Mrs Walker kept the next shop, it was a very select sweet shop. Against this was the Ram Inn, then the Palace picture house. On the front of the Palace was a small shop owned by Mr Moreton, he used to sell fruit and sweets. On Saturday afternoon he would secure a tray round his neck. It was filled with lots of sweets and he would go into the Palace selling them. I believe that the next shop was called Campion's which was a bicycle shop. After that was Mrs Moreton's fish and chip shop. Next came Mr Boyer's hardware, then Mr Alty Adcock's shop, he sold all kinds of furniture. There was then a very small sweet shop owned by Mrs Lawrence. Next came Mrs Mee's house facing Chapel Street, across the road from which was Mee's shop and bakery. I used to stand for ages looking at the iced cakes in the shop window. I had never had anything like them. The bakery was up the yard at the back of the shop. Mrs Mee was the mother of Douglas, Ellis and Ernie. I remember once that they opened the ovens on a Sunday morning for the people to take their Sunday meat to be cooked.

At that time there was no coal to be had, I don't know why as most of the men were miners. I know that we had to go into the fields to collect wood to make fires. I was very puzzled by that. Next to Mee's was a gents' shop owned by the Lawrences. Then came Holmes' boot and shoe shop, later it was Riley's. Next there were two houses and then Lloyd's drapery shop. I often went there for some calico for Mam to make us children chemises, as we did not have vests when I was a child. Then came a lovely cottage, where I believe that Mr Hopkins lived with his family. I also remember Miss Meek, the headmistress of the infant school, living there. After that came a row of cottages, then Crane's the butchers and then Mrs Hurst's fruit and sweet shop. Next was Harratt's house and up the yard, at the side, was the blacksmith's, owned by the Harratt brothers. I loved to go there, dad would send me with a pick helve, I think that's what it was called. I had to ask them to sharpen it. If they were busy I had to wait but I didn't mind as I loved to watch them at the forge, blowing the coal until it glowed. They would put some iron in it until it was red hot and then take it out and put it on the anvil. They would make sparks fly when they hammered it.

Across the yard from Harratt's house was a butcher's shop. I did not see that open many times. After that came a house, then Bayliss' pork butcher's shop, it smelled lovely in there. I remember he used to make pork pies and put them on the trays ready to take to Mee's bakery to be baked. They always looked wet to me and I found out later that they had been brushed with egg. Next door was a house, then Tyler's sweet shop. Then across a yard from that was Overton's fish and chip shop. After that came Mr and Mrs Trivit's sweet shop, they were a very nice couple. Next

16

was Allen's paper shop and across a yard from that another butcher's shop, I believe that the name was Allsop. There were then three more houses, then the jitty next to Clark's beer-off. I remember going there for a pint of beer for a neighbour and they put a label over the cork on the bottle. I suppose that was to make sure that I did not open it.

Next to Clark's was another butcher's shop that belonged to Mr and Mrs Preston, a dear old couple who celebrated their Diamond Wedding and I remember puzzling over that. I did not know until I was older what that meant. After that came Maria's, who I mentioned earlier. It must have been a one up one down house, it was so small. Next was another house and I remember Miss Hatton, the manageress of Ibstock Co-op drapery shop, lived there. Then came Mrs Richardson's shop, she sold all kinds of children's and ladies' clothes. Next came two more houses, then Newman's house, I believe that they had a small holding there, as they sold milk. After that was a big house with a lot of steps leading up to the front door. I don't know who lived there when I was small but as I grew older Mrs Smith took it over and made a hairdressing business there. Next was Worthington's grocery store and then the Whimsey public house, at the bottom of Gladstone Street - it was called Deacon's Lane in my day. Then came Smith's fish and chip shop, then two or three more houses, I do not know how many there were, then Bircher's yard. After those came Mr Eggington's newspaper shop. If I remember correctly, there was a drapery shop next door and, I believe, Mr Elson kept that. The Post Office came next, managed by Mr Ford.

The other side was a dolls' shop, which had all kinds of dolls in there, kept by Mrs Lane. Then there came the gates to the back of the Post Office. Then a big yard with a detached house in it. This belonged to the Jordan family. After that there more houses, next to a yard where two sisters had a coal-carting business. I was amazed at them, they must have been very strong. I believe that their name was Ison. Next came another house, then Narrow Lane. Across the bottom of the Lane was Nicoll's sweet shop, then another row of houses. Next was a yard, or driveway, in which a horse and carriage used to drive up. They belonged to a lady living in the big house. I believe that the lady's name was Miss Hind. I saw her being driven through the village once. I go by two more old fashioned houses, on the very corner of the High Street, then a minute's walk round another corner we come to another big house called The White House. I did not know who lived there. Next was Mr Wright's house, he was a teacher at our school. The children used to call him Daddy Wright. The children in his class told me that he gave you the cane for the least little thing. I dreaded going to school when it was my turn to be in his class. I need not have worried, I found him to be very nice. Anyway, he never gave me the cane.

There was another drive leading to a house but I didn't know who lived there. Next came Mr Eggington's cottage, I heard someone say that he was an Alderman. I walk across the bottom of Hall Lane to two more cottages, then lastly to the Crown Inn

17

public house. That completes the walk along the High Street.

The First World War finished when I was ten years old. I remember walking along the High Street waving a small Union Jack flag. Most people seemed to be doing the same thing. It was lovely to see people so happy. As I grew older I had a lot more work to do, such as scrubbing out the closet and swilling the floor. I also had to scrub the back kitchen, which had a lovely red floor and I loved to see the soap bubbles that I made when I scrubbed, to me they looked like beads. Mam had five children by this time and needed a lot of help.

I used to waken in the morning to the sound of punching. That was a neighbour's washday. She had the clothes in a wooden tub and was punching them with wooden punchers. If it was not her washday it would be the pig killer killing a pig. I'm glad that it is not allowed to happen now.

Sometimes, on a Saturday, a scissors grinder would come down our road and go to all the houses to see if anyone wanted anything sharpening. He would put them all together, fix up his grinder and start pedalling away. He sharpened knives and scissors. Once an organ grinder came down our road and I hoped that he would come again but he never did.

Once a year we had Ibstock Wakes and it was held in a field opposite the Crown Inn. People came from all the surrounding villages to take part. I think that it was Holland's fair that came but I can't be sure of that. Another event was the Flower Show which was held on the field where the Community College now stands. A Mr Kendall from Common Hill seemed to win most of the prizes.

There is another thing that springs to my mind. It is the fever hospital at the top of the next field to the reccy. We children had heard what a good time the children had in there, so we decided to go and see if we could catch Scarlet Fever. The children in there came to the fence to shout to us but we could not get close enough to them. We didn't catch the fever and there is now a pig farm in the place of the hospital.

Once a year Coalville Co-op gave a treat to all its members but it was held at Coalville, so we had to walk if we wanted to go to it. There was a brake that went from Ibstock but we couldn't afford to go in it. The brake consisted of a large cart with wooden seats on each side of it and there were two horses to pull it along. I imagine that we were better walking.

As I said before I was ten years old when the war finished and life went on just the same for the next few years. I left school at thirteen thinking that I would have a much better life when I started to work. Was I disillusioned? I am afraid that I was but that's another story.

18

George Moore

Ibstock in my younger days was a bustling, thriving and vibrant village. You always seemed to be part of the everyday life. They were also hard days, but you lived in a community that cared. Never much money to spare, the people of Ibstock made their own enjoyment.

From where I lived, moving down to the 'Stumps' from the Royal Oak (kept at the time I remember, by Mr Jordan, a cantankerous gentleman, who, if he spotted you in the Oak Field, would come bellowing with a horse-whip in his hand. We never used to stop to argue), the Town Hall was the first building at the side of Smith's Lane (Hall Street). Mrs Storer kept the shop on the corner, which was open seven days a week, and you could always knock on the door if she was closed. You then moved down Hinckley Road, where you smelt paraffin and wax from Mort Wilkins' shoe repair shop and paraffin seller. Just below the Crown Inn, kept by Mr Crane, was a row of stables at the rear. Opposite was St Denys Church and vicarage. The rector, one of the most loved of rectors, was Reverend Birke. After leaving the church, with the conker tree right in the middle of its great avenue of trees, you passed Locker's Lane. Then you were at the beginning of the heart of Ibstock.

On the corner of the High Street lived David Manton, painter and decorator, opposite a beautiful, old, wood-fronted Georgian house, right at the side of the road. You then passed Harrison's Yard, which took you by Arch Crane's farmyard at the rear of the farmhouse. Beyond this was beautiful open countryside, once you got over the brook. Next to Harrison's Yard was Dick Thirlby's grocery shop. A little further along was Dr Agnew's house. His surgery, I believe, was held in The Manor House, just inside Locker's Lane. Opposite was the Post Office. The telephone exchange was part of the Post Office. Lenny Mears was the blacksmith. His forge was between Thirlby's and Dr Agnew's house.

Another notable was Ted Black, who kept The Whimsey Inn. He ran the billiard hall over Worthington's shop, and had a boxing ring in a shed in the pub yard. J T Jacques lived at the Motts, a large house set back from High Street, with a drive down to the large front door. Another prominent family were the Harratts. They lived in, as we called it, Harratt's Yard. He was blacksmith, carpenter, joiner, and funeral undertaker. His daughter was I believe, one of my teachers at the Junior School.

The chemist's shop opposite was run by Mr Brownlow, and many a time I have been in to get small amounts of medicine, probably sixpenny worth, or as high as a shilling. He used to make all his own medicines up, and oils, ointments and pills.

Just below was the focal point of entertainment in Ibstock, The Palace. Silent films were shown, and we used, as children, to go to the Saturday afternoon matinee, which cost tuppence to go in. We sat on long wooden benches at the front with noses about a yard away from the screen. Alty Adcock used to play the piano for the silent films.

Sometimes a touring troupe would take over The Palace, and they also used to run the Saturday Bash, as we called it. When talking pictures came out, the first film saw was Al Jolson. As we grew older, we were allowed to go to The Palace at night Then we used to sit with the adults. Moreton's sweet shop was part of The Palace and it was a treat to get a pennyworth of sweets during the interval. Next to The Palace was Chaplin's fish shop. Fish and chips were then, I believe, fourpence portion. Both shops used to do a roaring trade.

Alty Adcock kept the music shop just below The Palace. Opposite this shop, on the corner of Chapel Street, was Geordy Cornwall's sweet shop. A somewhat eccentric character with a white goatee beard. You always got a good buy from Geordy. Two thatched cottages stood inside Chapel Street, next to Cornwall's shop. Further up Chapel Street was the Co-op. First was the butcher's shop, adjoining the grocer shop, then the haberdashery shop.

When I was old enough, I used to fetch a parcel of groceries every Thursday evening, all neatly packed in thick, brown paper and tied with string. My school clothes were nearly always bought from the haberdashery. I had stiff, celluloid collars that used to make my neck sore if they cracked. Collars, were always sold separately. Boots, gansies, shirts, stockings, short trousers were all stocked beside a host of other clothing. I believe a Miss Hatton was the manager of this department.

Opposite was Mr Fowkes, who kept the bicycle shop. If I remember rightly, Hercules cycle cost £3-19-6. I remember this as my friend, Jackie Ball, had one for Christmas, and it was on this that I learned to ride.

There were other notable people living in Ibstock at this time. Lawyer Newman solicitors, Newman's - family butchers and bakers, Mr Burchell - newsagent. Mr Iliffe, I believe, was the school bobby. Constable Potterton, a man who I have seen break up fights by just moving into them. The Eggington family was also prominent family. These were business people who made their living in Ibstock.

Carrying on along High Street, you came to Meadow Row, a large row of houses overshadowed in my time by Ibstock gasworks. This used to supply all the gas for Ibstock's needs, before electricity came to the village. It was then closed down and demolished.

Carrying on, you passed the cemetery on your left and then along the Bridle Path that brought you out at Ellistown Pit. Ibstock Colliery was working then, a pit that had a footrill so that you could walk straight into the mine from ground level. The narrow gauge railway lines also used to run part of the way alongside the Bridle.

Village social life was also varied. Christmas was a festive time to end the old year You hung your stocking on the bottom bed rail and Christmas morning you would probably find apples, oranges, sweets, and if you were lucky, a sixpenny piece or a shilling piece - even half-a-crown. Christmas dinner was always a family affair. I remember my Uncle Frank used to come for Christmas. We used to sit down for a dinner that would consist of cockerel, potatoes, greens and stuffing - all home grown bar the bird. This was followed by a large helping of Christmas pudding which had been made and boiled in the copper in the wash-house.

You made your own entertainment in those days. I remember my two aunts, one played the piano, the other the violin. There were also home-made mince pies and pork pie, all washed down by either beer from The Oak or home-made wine. My favourite was parsnip wine. Everything was turned into something in those days. Left-overs into stews, stale bread into bread pudding.

The next thing was the Sermons. Held in early May, this was, for us who attended, the time of the year for a new outfit of shoes, stockings, shirt with a soft collar and, if you were lucky, a new jacket to go with the rest. Ganzies were mostly worn by boys - equivalent to the pullover today. Each chapel used to compete to see who had the largest collection. A hundred pounds for chapel funds was the usual collection for both services. Boys and girls used to sit on raised tiers of planks. Five or six tiers of planks were used for the Sermons, for which all boys and girls who attended chapel had practised twice a week for a month. I believe Mr Godfrey and Mr Tommy Smith were the teachers that got us into singing. The chapel would be packed, afternoon and evening. It was a custom that, no matter what your denomination, you attended all sermons, including the church, ensuring a full house wherever it took place.

Following this was Prize-giving Day, where every child who attended the Methodist Chapel received a book prize. I know I had some great prizes. I remember I had Treasure Island one year, and I kept it for moments when I felt like a change from the comics I used to get. Chips, Wizard, Comic Cuts and Adventure were my weekly reading.

Easter Sunday was another day that Ibstock celebrated, with a large decorated parade. Horses and waggons, horses and riders and decorated motor vehicles. All the vehicles were packed with children. At the rear of these would be Ibstock United Band and leading dignitaries followed by Scouts Band, Scouts and Girl Guides, then the Chapel and Church members. I believe they used to finish up for a Morning Service at St Denys Church.

The next event for us was the Sunday School treat, sometimes held in Ibstock, but two or three times we went to Spring Hill at Whitwick, next to St Bernard's Monastery. This was always a good outing with refreshments at the farmhouse that stood at the bottom of the outcrop.

Sports Day at the school was another event which was enjoyed by pupils and spectators alike. The house who finished first in the sports, was awarded, I believe, The Tebbut Cup. I may be wrong, but anyway it was a feather in the house's cap which managed to win the cup.

One of the events after the summer holidays was The Wake. This was looked on as a chance for the family get-together. Again I know Uncle Frank never used to miss Wake Saturday and Sunday. My grandparents' house was always overflowing on this occasion. In my day it used to be held on the Oak Field, opposite where I lived. There used to be Holland's, Pearson's and Bishop's Amusements. During the week's stay, no matter what the weather, there was always a good attendance and very little trouble. If there was, you always had PC Potterton to sort things out. I also remember that some of these show people used to winter on the field until it was time to take to the road again. They never caused trouble and used the time to overhaul and repair their amusements. During their stay, some used to attend the Junior and Modern Schools. They were always a friendly bunch of people and we all used to get on well with them.

Then there came the time that all of my age looked forward to - leaving school. I left Ibstock Modern School at Christmas 1929 and started work at George Ward of Barwell. One of my aunts got me the job. I remember my first job was sorting heels and lasts out and putting them in their respective compartments. I went from that job to heel scoring, not a very pleasant job.

I left my grandfather's house in early 1931 and moved back to live with my mother at the rear of the Boot Inn in a small cottage that was not big enough for all of us to live decently. I left Ward's soon after leaving my grandparents, and took the plunge. As there were not many jobs around Ibstock, I went to work at Nailstone Pit. My uncle, Bob Gamble, lived at Strawberry Villa, alongside Pisca Lane and Melbourne Road. I was put on night shift with my uncle Bob and Bill Proudman of Battram. I shall always remember my first trip down Nailstone. I remember stepping onto the cage which dropped like a stone down the shaft. I thought I had left my stomach behind. A bigger shock awaited me when I was told to fetch a pit pony from the stables and go pony driving with my uncle and Bill. I had only an oil-filled cycle lamp, filled with Colzer oil, with a spare bottle to carry around, and a box of matches. The world I had opted for was wet, muddy and foul smelling. My uncle and Bill were working, at that time, down the South District, the furthest roadway from the coal face. It took me quite a while to get used to the conditions, especially when my pony used to play up. Believe it or not, a couple of times I had to rely on him to get me back to the pit bottom, when my lamp ran out of oil. There were times when I know I thought, "What the hell have I let myself in for?"

However, I had worked there for about a year all on night shift, for fourteen shillings for a forty hour week, which worked out at around fourpence ha'penny an hour but, at sixteen, it was a job. Then one night I was told to break in a new pony. I had trouble trying to put his tackle on, assisted by the hostlers, when he started kicking and rearing. He bolted out of the stable, turned onto the main road, and collided with an air door which opened the other way. He hit this and broke his neck. Before I went home, I was hauled before the manager who told me I was sacked. I tried to tell him what had happened, but he did not want to know. Then he said to me, "Get out of my office. Horses cost money, we get ****** like you for nothing." That was the attitude of your employer those days. If he had not run out of the office, I would have thumped him.

I got another job then at Ellistown, as a putter fetching tubs of coal from the stall and taking empty tubs in to be filled. I had not been there very long when they started sending us home early. The coal owners had imposed a quota on how much coal was required. If your face fitted, and you were well in with the Deputy, you stayed.

By this time, mother and the rest of us had moved from the small cottage to a new house on Leicester Road. Here I met up again with Jack Seager, who also worked at Ellistown and, like me, he was one of the first to be told to "Get your coat on and tally out." This reduced your wages and stopped you getting a small amount of money from the Dole Exchange.

Jack and I packed in Ellistown Pit and I got a job at Desford Pit. After a short while, the same thing happened there. Sometimes I was allowed to stay and sometimes had to go. Then, I remember, they used to use South Pit whistle to tell you if you were not to work the following day. This used to blow, I believe, at 6pm with a long blast. This meant you were not working the next day. The only trouble was, if you had not heard it owing to the wind in the wrong direction, you biked to work next morning, to be told, "The pit's off," so you had biked to Desford at 6am to start work, only to be told to go back home.

There came a time when I had had enough of this messing about, and in 1934 I joined the army as a Regular. Even at ten shillings per week, I was better off financially. I served in Ireland, India and the Far East. I went to India in 1936 and came back to Ibstock in 1945. I remember my home-coming quite well. My mother had remarried. She had married one of my uncles, Uncle Dick. After meeting some of my relatives, I told my mother I was going out for a drink, but I was in for a shock. No pubs were open. So I decided to take a walk. I went down Locker's Lane, intending to turn down Belcher's Bar, just topside two thatched cottages that stood on the cross roads to Odstone. I kept on walking, then suddenly realised I was down to Grassy Lane. I would not have known then, if it had not been for a gypsy caravan parked there. I turned around and made my way back until I got to the cross roads, and walked down Belcher's Bar. My mother was worried because I had been gone so long. My mother then told me that the cottages had been demolished. Next morning I put some civvies on and took a walk around Ibstock. Starting at the Church, up Melbourne Road to the ballusole rubbish tip, I turned around along Leicester Road, down to Meadow Row and back down High Street. Nothing had hardly changed since I left Ibstock in 1936. A few new names on the shops, one or two houses missing, but all the pubs still there. A lot of familiar faces and plenty I did not know. A word here and there, and a feeling that I was back home at last. 'A very, very lucky man'.

S Wallace

My first recollection of doing anything in Ibstock was of going to the Infant School, which was, at that time, situated in Grange Road. It was quite often called School Fields because, if you continued to the end of Grange Road, it did eventually lead into fields, with footpaths leading in various directions, which people walked when they felt inclined.

The headmistress at the Infant School in my time was Miss Meek. I don't remember all the other teachers but two I do. They were Mrs Spiller, a rather large lady, and Miss Knight. Both of these teachers lived in Ibstock. As far as I can recall the time seemed to pass pleasantly enough during the two years that I spent there.

It was on the fields at the bottom of Grange Road that we had our recreation ground or 'reccy' as we called it. This was equipped with two lots of swings, one larger than the other, and a see-saw. These were used by children of both sexes but, by far, the majority of the field was used by boys playing at football. There were no goal posts as such, so goals were made by boys putting their coats on the ground. The distance between them was just paced out so arguments sometimes ensued, especially when high shots were sent in, as to whether the ball went over or under the non-existent cross bars. Generally speaking, a good time was had by all. All players were dressed in their ordinary clothes and boots so occasionally, in bad weather, we returned home somewhat dirtier than our parents would have liked. I distinctly remember the swimming pool, close to the brook, which had dirty water in it. It had no roof and I have no memory of seeing anybody paddling in it. It was later pulled down and never replaced.

Children from the Infant School transferred to the school at the top of Grange Road. This was known, at the time, as The National School.

One gentleman, who lived in Grange Road, was the Town Crier, Mr Richard Gray, or Dickie Pepper as most people called him. He was, indeed, the person who did that particular job. I remember him walking along the street of the village making the announcements when he was required to do so. He carried a bell with which he summoned attention to what he had to announce, in very loud tones. I also remember that he had a kind of uniform when on his legitimate business. I don't remember anyone else doing the job after he did it.

The National School was quite large and pupils went there until the school leaving age, which was then thirteen. Some pupils from this school took examinations to transfer to the Grammar Schools in the area. There were three of these, Coalville, Ashby-de-la-Zouch and Market Bosworth. It must be remembered that when pupils went to the end of their time in The National School they were able to officially go to work.

The headmaster of The National School was Mr Dunstan, who was also organist at the Parish Church. It was, at the time, a joint position of headmaster and church organist.

The Infant School was eventually closed in Grange Road and new premises were built on Melbourne Road, adjacent to the Council School which was built in 1906. This is the present Junior School. From this pupils transferred to the Community College, which was built in the 1920s; it was originally called Ibstock Secondary Modern School but has been added to over the years to become a Community College. There is now a fine up-to-date swimming pool which opens, at certain times, to the general public. Pupils either transfer to the Grammar School or leave to start work.

There were, in the early part of this century, two railways in the area. One ran from Loughborough to Nuneaton, passing along the valley between the hills which take you into and out of Heather. We had to walk to the station unless we were fortunate enough to obtain a ride in a farm's cart. This railway ran along to Shackerstone and Market Bosworth and other stations beyond. There was a junction at Shackerstone where you changed trains to take you to Ashby-de-la-Zouch.

I, along with quite a number of boys from Ibstock, travelled on this train when we all attended the Dixie School in Market Bosworth. The only other way to travel this five miles to school was to cycle, which, I remember, everybody did as time went on. This line was closed down in 1931. The other line ran from Burton-on-Trent to Leicester. This used to be the best way to travel to Leicester in my very early years. I very well remember being taken to Bagworth Station to board the train there. There were two ways of getting to Bagworth, one being by horse drawn brake which travelled there every Saturday. Two people, I remember, ran these vehicles, Cherry's of Chapel Street and Newbold's of Curzon Street. Cherry's used to run to Bagworth every Saturday morning to catch the first train to Leicester. The other means of getting to Bagworth was to walk up Pretoria Road - quite often called Common Hill - then along the pathway to the top end of Ellistown (as we called it) and then to Bagworth Station. This walk had to be repeated in the opposite direction on the return journey. The age of the car and bus was still to come. For people who wished to attend Coalville Market a brake was available on Friday afternoons.

Street lighting during this period of time was by gas. We had our own gas works, which was situated at the bottom of Pretoria Road. It was built in 1871 and functioned until 1950. Gas lamps were in various places around the village. It was a common sight to see an employee of the gas works cycling around with a long pole which he used to reach up and put on the lamps to full power, when the appropriate time came to do so. Coke was also available as a fuel, from the gas works, and villagers went there, mostly at week-ends, with barrows and other means of taking it away to their homes. The gas works finally closed down when our lighting was converted to electricity and our domestic gas came from another source.

When I eventually left school in 1923, I obtained my first job at Ibstock Colliery as a clerical worker. The 1926 General Strike was a cloud over the whole country and the colliery was forced to close down, putting many people out of a job. I was one of many and, due to the state of the country, it was just about impossible to obtain alternative work. I have to admit this was not a particularly pleasant time and everybody was glad when the strike ended. The colliery closed down two years later and miners were able to find situations at other local collieries. I managed to obtain other work in Loughborough.

A person I must mention during these years was our village carrier, Mr Tom Dawson. Apart from running a small holding, twice a week he travelled to Leicester with a horse and cart carrying and fetching parcels. The days he went were Wednesday and Saturday. The journey took him all day. When he gave up he was followed by two gentlemen - brothers-in-law - Wood and Johnson. They did the work by a motor lorry. I don't remember anybody else doing the job after they gave up.

It was during these years that motor transport began to grow. I do remember when there were only three private vehicles in the village, two doctors and a local businessman. This was soon to change as the number of vehicles began to grow. In place of the aforementioned brakes we soon had five fleets of buses - Messrs Hipwell, Ruden, Windridge, Sons and Riley, Bircher Brothers and Fowkes. One of their chief occupations was to take people to their daily work in Leicester, Barwell and Earl Shilton. At other times regular services were set up to Leicester and Coalville. Trips were also organised to travel to seaside resorts and places of interest all around the country. This enabled the villagers to travel about more than they had previously been able to do. By now, the railways had closed down and have not, as yet, been replaced.

During the early years of this century the Palace Cinema was built by the Wain Brothers, who lived in Station Road. In the early years a matinee was held on Saturday afternoons for children. The cost, as far as I can remember, was tuppence per head. The noise when we had a Cowboys and Indians film was terrible, especially when they did battle for something or other. The Palace was open every night for adults and I remember people queueing up to get in. The cinema ran for quite a number of years until it stopped showing pictures and changed into a Bingo Hall. For some months it has been For Sale.

Also, in the early years, whist drives and dances were held in The National School, mostly for charitable purposes. My memories of these were of being taken by my parents on Saturday nights. They were whist players and I remember being in the room where the dancers were. I was fascinated watching all the young grown-ups performing their dances. It was a very colourful sight. Supplying the music for these nights were Alty Adcock and Fred Brown, who were both pianists. That was the only music at that time. I remember thinking that I would like to be able to dance and when I became a teenager I learned to do so.

During this time we had our own local dance band in the village - The Broadway Syncopators as they were named. Mr Fred Brown was the pianist, two of the Mee bothers, Ernest and Ellis, played drums and banjo, plus a violinist who was imported. The Mee brothers were of the baker family and lasted quite a number of years until finally retiring from the fray. I had many pleasant evenings, along with others, doing the light fantastic. No other band took their place. Now dancing is still carried on in the Working Men's Club on Saturday nights.

A society which ran at this time was the Debating Society. This was a Society mainly for men except on a few special occasions. This was run on parliamentary lines on Monday evenings, in the Town Hall. The hall was situated on Melbourne Road at the top of Hall Street.

The procedure was for two members to choose a subject of their own, one would put forward his reasons for the topic, as it was called, and the other against. A vote was taken at the end, after other speakers had expressed their preference for one of the speakers. I first attended with my father in my early teens. There was no compulsion to speak but members were expected to do so. After attending for some time it was my turn to make a speech. This I did with some degree of nervousness. I'm sure it did help to put your thoughts into reasonable English and also to appreciate other members' points of view. The Society ran until the beginning of World War II, when the hall closed down to become an air raid base. The Society did not start again after the war and the hall was eventually taken down for road widening.

Another society which came into being a little over forty years ago was the Townswomen's Guild. They have speakers to address them and any funds raised go to different charities. They also put on a public concert once a year which can be attended by both sexes. The concert usually consists of songs and sketches. The sketches are usually very humorous and create a great deal of fun.

Years ago concerts were put on at one or other of the chapels but these have long ceased to take place. Now, occasionally, some form of entertainment is put on at the Working Men's Club. I don't think we have the amount of entertainment in the village that we used to have. Perhaps the advent of television has had some influence on that. Maybe the future will bring new things as the years go by.

My Early Memories of Ibstock by D Middleton

I was born in Ibstock in June 1927. We lived for the first seven years in East Walk, near the High School entrance.

One of my earliest memories is of picking dandelions for making wine. The older girls took us smaller children down the Heather Fields and onto the Ballast Hole where we picked the flower heads. We took them home and tipped them into the copper belonging to the lady next door, who made the wine.

Other recollections are of walking to Nailstone across the fields, at a very tender age, to visit Grandma. We continued to walk there most weeks until she died in 1938.

I can also remember men being brought home from the pits injured, my own father included. They were covered in blood and coal dust, lying on straw in a horse-drawn float.

Living near the monument, I can remember the Armistice days of that time. The older boys were marched out from the senior school where they, and the other mourners, gathered in a circle around the monument. Any tradesmen about at that time, i.e. bakers, milkmen, etc. would alight from their vehicles and stand with heads bowed, to observe one minute's silence, as did other people on the streets. I can also remember a horse-drawn funeral taking place in West Walk, the horses had black plumes on them.

We seemed to spend a lot of time sitting on the kerb in New Road (officially Central Avenue) rolling 'bossy' marbles and screwing tops into gaps. We would see miners biking home from work with their white snap bags on their arms. There would also be an occasional bus belonging to Hipwell's or Windridge's passing by.

In 1934, we moved to Ashby Road where my Father had a new house built. On looking back, it must have been a dicey thing to do as miners' work was very spasmodic. The miners would listen for the buzzer to sound at a certain time to know if they should report for work or not. In those pre-war days they must have had a lot of free time, when there was no work. Dad would make us a kite and help to fly it, another time he made us a sledge.

Mum and Dad would meet my brother and myself out of school to go picking blackberries. We would also walk to Normanton Wood to look for wild raspberries. We used to walk as a family, including aunts and uncles. We would go over the fields to Shackerstone, to swim in the canal and picnic, sometimes calling at The Rising Sun Inn on the way back for pop and crisps. What a treat. We also walked to Ravenstone Mill. This was nearer to Ibstock than Ravenstone. It was a beautiful place with its mill pond and mill race. It was a shame that in later years it was allowed to fall into decay and has now disappeared completely under the opencast mining.

Not many ordinary people had holidays away then, as they do nowadays. Bardon Hill was another favourite place for us to visit. It was a lovely walk up from Bardon Chapel. The hill side was covered in trees and there was a sort of summer house at the top. Whichever way we walked, we would meet other families that we knew.

Every boy, in those days, had a hoop to bowl along. We used to go straight down Melbourne Road (very little traffic about), hitting the hoop with a stick. It was the same with whip and top. We stuck the top into a hole, wound the string round and would be off down the road. All the girls had a big skipping rope and had a great time in the school playground and at home.

Cowboys and Indians was popular with the boys. This was the result of our weekly visit to the Saturday matinee at Ibstock Palace, usually costing us two pennies. Before the picture show we would call at Baker's shop near the end of Central Avenue for a ha'penny bag of monkey nuts or Moreton's shop near the Palace for sweets. If we were feeling very brave we went into George Cornwall's shop (strictly forbidden by parents), this was nearly opposite the Palace, at the bottom of Chapel Street. The shop window was always decorated with nice-looking hams, cooked meats, etc. but sometimes you could see white mice walking about. It was a fascinating place if you dared go in. Some of the braver boys would go in to buy a piece of cake, always cut off a large cake, usually pink.

Mr Cornwall always wore a chef's hat. He had a goatee beard and was small and dapper. The boys would rile him up and he would chase them out of his shop waving a knife or cleaver. For the 1937 Coronation, he decorated the shop with flags and bunting, photos, including ones of the King and Queen and one of himself and underneath each one was a placard saying 'King George, Lloyd George and little George Cornwall'. His normal sign read 'George Cornwall, Professional Chef and Cook'.

The corner of Chapel Street was much sharper then and many bikes failed to take the bend and ended up in Alty Adock's window.

Round about the age of eight years I joined Ibstock Parish Church choir, my brother being already a member. We had gone to church and Sunday School from earliest days, as did most of the children in Ibstock, either church or chapel. Once you had joined the choir you stayed until your voice broke; it was hard work but we also had some fun. The Rector at that time was the Reverend Newbery, the choirmaster and organist was Mr Handford from Coalville. Mr Handford was a man to be respected and feared. He was a perfectionist and an organist of some repute. Choir practice would go on and on until we got it right. If you lost interest he would soon throw something at or near to you to wake you up.

The organ then was the old type with hand-pumped bellows. If you had to stand in for Mr Sammy Knifton, the regular man on the bellows, woe betide the boy who did not watch the little mouse on the string and let him run out of air. I have never seen anyone play like Mr Handford. Nothing went on behind him without him knowing.

He could turn and glare at you whilst playing the most difficult tune. Mind you, about fifteen boys needed some watching.

Nevertheless, we had some good times on outings to other churches and places. One Saturday, September 2nd 1939, we choirboys were taken, by the Reverend Newbery and Mr Handford, to London by train and a great time was had by all. There must have been a lot of black-faced boys walking about that day as we spend most of the journey with our heads stuck out of the train windows. We saw lots of sights in London, including some of Sir Oswald Moseley's followers being marched away for the duration of the war under Order 18 B, as they called it.

Wherever we went we marched in file. I remember everywhere was being sand-bagged up but the biggest shock was on our return home. An evacuee from Birmingham, a nine year old boy called Raymond Cuddy, had arrived to live with us.

At the following Sunday morning service the Reverend Newbery left the church, I assume to listen to the wireless, because he came back and stood on the chancel steps and told us that war had been declared.

Back to schooldays - I have happy memories of the infants school in Grange Road, with Miss White as headmistress. After that I moved up to the junior school on Melbourne Road with Mr Horace Harratt as headmaster. He ruled us with a firm hand. In the mornings the boys and girls lined up for inspection, like a military parade. He would walk down the lines, both back and front, checking that boots were clean and shiny. All the boys wore short trousers until their first or second year at the senior school, we also wore studded boots. These were great for making slides halfway across the school playground in the winter.

I remember an earlier trip to London with the school before the church trip. We went from Heather Station to Chalk Farm Station in London and from there to London Zoo. It was a great day out.

When the war started I was at the senior school and it soon altered our lives. With the large influx of evacuees, mostly from Birmingham, we boys were kept busy taking out bedding for them. This was picked up on handcarts from the Toc H rooms. I must say, at this point, that many former evacuees still keep in touch with their host families.

As the war went on teachers left to join the armed forces. We boys were kept busy digging most of the available land at the school for vegetable growing. We also dug a small field at the back of the Pretoria Road allotments. In addition to this, both boys and girls wrote the addresses on ration books for Market Bosworth Rural District Council. The girls were also kept busy making jams and preserves.

An incident I remember well from my senior school days was when some boys were reported to Mr Measures, a strict headmaster, for using bad language. This was as they travelled on a bus from one of the outlying villages. The headmaster told the whole school that the boys were to be punished and they would witness the punishment. The boys were led into a washroom where basins had been filled with soapy water. The boys were made to wash their mouths out with this. Then they were taken into the main hall and given six strokes of the cane by Mr Measures.

The difference in Ibstock from the days before the war and after are tremendous. Previously, there were eight or nine farms around the village. The people and the place were much more rural. Cattle and horses were seen daily in the streets. All the lads had trucks to collect manure for which dad paid a few pennies. We must have had more milkmen than many places, I can think of seven. I can remember Lyn Redshaw nipping along the Black Path from his cowshed at the start of the Heather Fields to his home on Melbourne Road, with his milk pails hanging from a wooden yoke on his shoulders. Many miners and boys helped out on the farms. Ibstock had a lot of characters, like George Street, plumber, painter and decorator. He had a walrus moustache and rode a bike with a double crossbar. The older people were always reciting the tales that he told. There was also David Manton, plumber, painter and handyman. He was quite a small man but in his yard he kept the longest ladders that I have ever seen. Mr Mears was the blacksmith, he had his forge in the High Street. He was also not very tall but he managed to shoe horses of all types, including Shires. Harratt's Yard was a marvellous place for boys. They made carts and coffins, shod horses and sawed up trees. All very good to watch when taking Dad's pick blades to be sharpened.

I also recall the church parades of years ago. They were big, with many people attending. There would be three Ibstock bands taking part, sometimes guest bands or the T.A. in the old uniform with puttees, etc. All the Friendly Societies took part, some of them on horseback.

A collection was always taken for the Leicester Royal Infirmary. The 1935 Jubilee and the 1937 Coronation were celebrated with torchlight processions and bonfires. These were wonderful events for school children to take part in. Earlier in the day we had entered fancy dress parades.

Another big do in the year was the annual Co-op Treat. If your parents were members you obtained tickets from the shop. Only children were allowed to travel, so off we went to Heather Station and caught the special train to Coalville East Station. There we joined up with other children and set off behind the 'Snibby' Band. We walked to a field near the slaughterhouse at Ravenstone turn. As you went in you were handed a bag of buns, cakes and sandwiches. My biggest worry was how I was going to find Mum and Dad in all that crowd, as they made their own way there. During the afternoon and evening we enjoyed the fun of the fair, a Punch and Judy Show and watched men trying to climb a greasy pole. There were races for children and adults and lots of other things to do. It was a great day out for the area.

As I write this and think back, it is hard to believe how we boys used to travel about covering quite a large area, mostly on bikes. It just shows the difference in our society today and, of course, there was very little traffic about. Incidentally, I bought the bike myself with earnings from errands and taking papers round.

Every aircraft that came down, and every bomb, we would be off to have a look. Looking back to the autumn and winter of 1940 when German bombers came over nightly, in the beginning we were quite frightened. It was eerie to hear that funny drone of the aircraft, they mostly went towards Derby then were driven away from there.

When they bombed Coventry we went with Dad, who was A.R.P. warden, down to Pisca Lane, nearly to where Parkdale is today, and from there you could see Coventry burning.

Forgive me for wandering a little in my reminiscences but I must mention the Wake. Fairs that came to Ibstock for the Wake in October time were a grand affair. Big steam traction engines gleamed with brass work. How they got into the Ram field between the cinema and the pub was a feat to behold.

The Ram field was home to Ibstock Cricket Club at one time. I spent quite a few Saturday afternoons there with Dad watching them play. I saw Larry Gains play there once.

The Hastings Arms field was the home of the Penistone Rovers football team. Everyone local knew that they were very good, and a large crowd always turned out to watch them.

During the war quite a few of the soldiers stationed at Gopsall Park used to visit the village, mostly for a drink at the Ram Inn. Often a few bikes would go missing in the evenings, the soldiers having 'borrowed' them to get back to Gopsall.

After the war things moved slowly for a start. The pits were nationalised but coal was still tipped outside homes in the street, in one ton loads. Hipwell buses were sold to Brown's Blue, house building started and today Ibstock is a very large place and, I should imagine, that sometime in the 1960s the day arrived, with the building of Valley Estate, etc. when Ibstock people no longer knew everyone in the village. Up to that time most did, even in our large village. You can pass people everywhere today and not know a soul. Some good things have happened here. The Community Centre is bound to be a plus and when we built the swimming pool the true Ibstock spirit came to life. My family, with others, decorated lorries, etc. for the fund-raising events and really enjoyed it. People only need a good cause to respond to. Fund-raising of recent years has proved this.

We are still called a village, we still keep our own history and identity and I hope as the years pass that they keep each village intact and green land between towns and villages. We still have a band that carries the Ibstock name and also football and cricket clubs. Our village name travels daily the length and breadth of the land on Ibstock Brick Yard lorries, delivering Ibstock bricks all over the country.

Frances Davies

Born and brought up in Ibstock, a terraced cottage in Chapel Street was my home, it was so comfortable and cosy. Dad, a miner, Mum, a dressmaker, Granny, a nurse and midwife, my sister and myself. Mum was born in the cottage and lived there the whole of her life. She married the lad next door and continued to live there with Granny. There was nothing they could not do - cooking, sewing, decorating, everything. The education at the National School (now a factory) on High Street was absolutely amazing.

Back to the cottage - washday was always Monday, in an outside wash-house. Five families used the same entry and shared wash-houses and pan lavatories, before the sewer was connected. At one time there were seventeen children out of the five houses leaving for school each day and mothers never had a wry word. Trestle tables were borrowed from the Baptist Chapel for birthday parties, all the children and friends had to come - all on the long back yard.

Bath night was Friday - Dad had a bath every day. A large pegged rug on the hearth in the small kitchen and water ladled out of the fireside boiler (ours had no tap). A large piece of hessian covered the cosy pegged rug - extra water had to be carried across from the wash-house and all the water had to be ladled out of the big zinc bath and carried outside and down two steps to the wash-house drain.

Our toilet was shared by two other families, who lived in the two houses which were down the step from ours. It had a twin seat and two pans! The two houses at the top of the yard also shared a toilet and wash-house. One lady washed on Monday and one on Tuesday. One of these ladies had nine children. They had two small bedrooms and two small rooms downstairs - no conservatory - the back door opened straight into the kitchen. We had two small downstairs rooms but, for some reason, our house had all the room upstairs over the entry. We were fortunate and had three bedrooms, decent sizes, and a landing with a closet at the end, my great-granny, I remember, being there too. I was four and a half when she died. Just before she died she had taken in a lodger, who was 21, for a fortnight because his landlady had bronchitis and he was with us until he died aged 85. He worked as a representative for Heather Brickyard (Ford's yard) and belonged to the Burslem family of Woods - potters. I have memories of the cosiness and the marvellous work carried on in these little houses. They were really homes.

The fun we all had as children there often comes flooding back. There was no such word as 'bored'. We all had our friends dotted about the village, we were always going and coming and playing for hours and hours. My special friend and I, from about the age of nine onwards, took other people's children out for walks all round Belcher's Bar and Heather. If we did not want to walk we took the children we had collected into my friend's orchard and paddock and entertained them up there. Some of their mums gave us a penny or two, odd ones - richer ones - gave us sixpence. We saved all these pennies and when we went to Grammar School bought hockey sticks, shoes, tennis racquets, etc. thereby helping our mums out. I bought a box camera for eleven shillings, a No: 2 Brownie, that is still going strong. We played lots of games, snobs, hide and seek, cricket, rounders, and we skipped and played ball for hours. We did errands for countless people. One in particular, Mrs Thirlby, who I called 'auntie' was a junior school teacher. She was a cousin of my gran, and was a fantastic person. She ran the church Sunday School. Whilst she was superintendent it topped 500 scholars! There were four bible classes, even some married people still went as they were so interesting. Out of all this number, if one was away this good 'auntie' got up early on the Monday morning to go to their houses to see why they had not been to Sunday School.

Mrs Heggs, Mrs Perry and Mrs Thirlby - Skegness 1920s

Dad's grandad and, I suppose, his great-grand parents, too, kept the toll bar at Belcher's Bar and lived in the cottage there.

Our Sunday School 'treats' were a yearly event and held in a field called 'The Four Leaves', just off Overton Road at the bottom of Harrison's Yard. These were enjoyed by all the Sunday School scholars - games, races, etc. and a tea.

At the bottom of Chapel Street and High Street, Georgie Cornwall, who'd been a chef in the navy, kept a very small shop selling cooked meat, sweets, etc. We used to go in there often with our Friday pennies (a week's pocket money) and sometimes buy a gob stopper for a whole penny. This stopped us talking and lasted for a whole week-end. Sometimes the children in the queue had four aniseed balls for a halfpenny. After all our friends were served, I was often last. George, instead of putting the bottle back on the top shelf for the last few in the queue, would say, "I suppose you want four?" "No," I would say and back went the bottle to its resting place on the top shelf. "Well, what do you want then, Frances?" "I want eight aniseed balls, please!" He ran us all out of his shop then. We all had respect and manners, too.

Dad, who was the baby of eleven, had an older sister Louisa who went out to work at thirteen years of age and her first job was with a family named Swan, who farmed at Odstone Hill Farm. They all had a family pew service at Ibstock on Sunday mornings, and everyone had to go. One day she took the lady of the house to the bank in Market Bosworth, up the hill to Belcher's Bar, in a donkey cart with Aunt Louisa driving. At the top of the hill the donkey refused to go any further and then a miner walking home from one of the collieries said, "Won't it move, m'duck? Pick a bit of that gorse and tickle it under its tail." By this time she was crying, thinking she would have her 'cards' (she already had her apron rolled up ready and the bunch of keys wrapped up inside). Anyway, she tried this trick and the donkey flew round and round in the road then back to the farm with Auntie trailing behind crying. When she arrived back at the farm the rest of the family stood at the front door watching the old lady in the cart tearing round the stock yard. Auntie laughed and laughed every time she told this story to anyone until she died at 93.

Dad's oldest brother Alf also had his story. He also left school at thirteen and he worked at Rowell's Farm down Overton Road until he was old enough to become an engine driver. He drove The Flying Scotsman for a number of years. One day, returning to the farm after lunch, he turned round in Overton Road and saw an elephant behind him. He ran as fast as he could and darted into the cottage up the hill. Mrs Ball lived in that cottage then. He ran into the kitchen and shut the door quickly, shouting, "Oh! Mrs Ball there's an elephant behind me." She laughed at him and opened the door to look and there was the elephant emptying her swill tubs. Anyway, the man from the travelling circus caught up with it then and everything was alright again.

During the war my friend and I did the 'Red Cross Penny-a-Week', collecting in Chapel Street every week during the war and for two or three years after the war. We ran a savings group with it - imagine the work - we never had a spare minute. We had loads of fun, though we were teased galore by many of the people - characters living there who we got to know very well.

During the war evacuees came to the village. One brother and sister came with a label attached to them, which said 'Please don't part them if you can help it'. They had to be parted as there was not a suitable billet left for them to be together. Keith was taken by one of the W.V.S. ladies for a couple of nights and my mum brought Betty for a couple of nights. No billet was found for them together. Keith stayed for the duration with a couple who had a son the same age and we kept Betty for six years. She stayed a year longer than she need have done so that her schooling was not interrupted and she could take the 11 plus. After going to grammar school in Birmingham she trained as a nurse and then went off to New Zealand nursing. Then she married out there and had four children. We have never lost touch and have visited her parents regularly over the years. They had a bungalow in North Wales where they holidayed for years and years and so did we. Betty has been over five or six times, sometimes with her husband. Her children have all been, except one, to visit their grandparents and us and all their relations. Sadly, her dad died about four years ago and her mum died last July, aged 93. We had marvellous times over the years.

Keith, her brother, billeted with Mr and Mrs Buckingham and their son, Herbert, had an interesting story too. He went home to Birmingham when he was eleven years old to go to grammar school. Then, doing his National Service, he met Herbert again, down at Portsmouth and again in Hong Kong. Then Herbert lodged with Keith's parents when he went to Birmingham University. They were best men for each other and, after they married, they lived in the same street in Northfield.

Early Recollections of Ibstock by Frank Gregory

During the war, about 1943, the word reached Ibstock like wildfire that people were coal picking on Nailstone Wood pit bank. It was mainly just a mountainous tip of waste slag but the shortage and high price of fuel turned ordinary people into coal prospectors. A school chum and I joined them up the slippery slopes on several week-ends, digging for nuggets of reject coal. Scores of people swarmed over the steep bank. Nobody seemed to realise the danger of landslides. My school friend and I journeyed many times from Nailstone pit to our homes in Ibstock pulling our groaning hand-truck.

Inevitably, the crunch came when the Coal Company erected hostile notices to stop the picking. We didn't think it fair, not after they'd thrown the coal away! Poor quality or not, our pig loved it. We always had a pig. This one attained a good old weight before it was slaughtered. Grandad said, "A lump of coal is good for it." So my immature mind concluded, the more the merrier. It's a wonder the bacon wasn't black!

Many people kept a pig before the war. Most back yards included a sty as normal procedure. We had one down Overton Road. The slaughterer came and did his work on your premises. Sometimes two families shared a pig because it took a lot of feeding. We used to boil the pig-potatoes and waste vegetables in an old coal-fired copper. You could smell hot potatoes for miles. Then kids would appear from nowhere, the signal for a feast.

Our low oak beams were the frequent bearers of hams and bacon cured with saltpetre rubbed into the flanks. They hung from hooks in the living room and we used to duck our heads under them. We had no fridge. The nearest thing to a fridge was a small container called a safe which was a box made of fine galvanised gauze to keep out the flies. At mealtimes Grandad would reach up, unhook a joint, carve off what we needed and then replace it on the ceiling hook. I suspect the meat was too salty for the flies, anyway.

Washday took up the whole of Mondays. Grandma would pound the clothes in a zinc tub with her copper-headed dolly, then feed them through this monster cast iron mangle. It was the size of a king-sized upright piano. It's funny how the most insignificant incident sticks in your mind. I was caught cracking hazel nuts in the large wooden rollers. Every year I enjoyed collecting hazel nuts from the nearby hedgerows. After a ripening period I'd impatiently crack a few. One of the rollers had a handy dent in it, which proved ideal for lodging the nuts in - until I was painfully dissuaded by a descending hand.

As we lived in a remote spot, Grandma set her clothes line out in the adjacent field where there was unlimited breeze, well away from our garden, which contained fruit trees and kidney bean sticks to snag the washing. Unfortunately, the cattle grazed this field and on occasion saw us chasing after half-dressed cows. Many of our shirts and blouses became firmly impaled on the horns of the beasts. Nothing was more daunting than the sight of Grandma in full flight, fists raised, chasing after her fast retreating bloomers. Next came the ironing and the starching of cuffs and collars. No mean job because Grandma first had to ensure a smokeless, well-stoked fire, even in the height of summer. She'd place two flat irons on a trivet close to the glowing fire bars. Every so often one was tested for temperature by dropping a globule of water on the upturned face. If the hissing liquid danced around and vaporised, the iron was ready for use. By this time the handle had become so unbearably hot that a very thick insulating pad was needed to pick it up.

Our Harold was called up to serve in the Forces, May 1940. He joined the Royal Air Force and narrowly missed serious injury when he was bombed at Newmarket. He chose not to report his injuries because he dearly wanted to be posted to South Africa with his mates. Unfortunately, his old wounds deteriorated and after about two years abroad they sent him back to Blighty on a hospital ship. He was discharged in April 1945. After several operations he eventually had to have the troublesome leg amputated in 1949.

Before the war Harold was a founder member of the Rainbow Accordion Band. Maurice Blazer was in charge. Maurice also gave piano accordion lessons for a small fee to people in their homes including our Harold and Audrey Talbott. The

Rainbow Accordion Band toured local village halls and was very popular but in 1939 Hitler spoilt it all and the band was split up. Young people had to join the Forces - or do a key job, like working down the mine. After the war the group never managed to get together again.

The break-up was particularly sad for me because they took me on their rounds of local concerts while still at Infants School. I soon learnt to knock simple tunes out of my little melodeon at this very tender age. They had a miniature uniform made for me and I joined them on stage - a sort of mascot. While the 'band proper' rested their fingers I was allowed a solo spot playing simple things like, 'Little Old Lady Passing By' and 'Horsey, Horsey Don't You Stop'. For this they saw I was well catered for with crisps and pop - and I always came away a few coppers richer. The band was quite big. They wore silky uniforms, red top, blue trousers with ridiculously wide bell-bottoms but the audience loved them.

There were many good marching bands parading in Ibstock before the Second World War. The Red Garries Carnival Band was one of Ibstock's finest. It was formed by Mr Arthur Mee and consisted mainly of teenagers. They played kettle drums, piano accordions and bazookas as they pompously marked in the long procession of Ibstock's big parades. I can hear them still, playing in perfect harmony on the march. When they reached the carnival field they gave superb displays, marching and playing, with the girl at the head showily twirling her stick, occasionally throwing it as high as the bedroom windows - and catching it on the march. The girls' uniforms consisted of white blouses and short gingham skirts.

Peggy Andrews and Peggy Mee were accordionists, marching side by side in the Red Garries Carnival Band. Miss Mee was the daughter of Arthur Mee, the organiser.

Although our Harold came out of the war with a gammy leg, that didn't stop him setting up a mobile fish and chip van in 1945. He bought a battered old lorry and converted it himself. A second-hand coal-fired cooking range was removed from a derelict chip shop and we fitted it in his vehicle. I was thirteen at the time and considered it fun to help out, which was welcomed. He later bought a more reliable ex-army lorry from Ruddington ex-army sales and transferred the van body from the old one.

Harold Talbott's Chip Van

He had a big round of villages to cater for - Higham-on-the-Hill, Stoke Golding, Dadlington, Newbold Verdon and Bagworth, to name a few. We used to stoke up the coal fires in the back of the van before we left Ibstock. One night we were motoring towards our first village stop when the fat overheated, swilled over the pan sides and burst into flames. Fortunately, we managed to rake out the fires and save the van from being gutted.

When I was old enough Harold fixed L plates to the chip van for me to drive while he prepared for frying. He lived at Church View, in a prefabricated concrete bungalow at the time, but kept the van at Grandma's house down Overton Road. Some Saturdays saw me driving to Bagworth railway station to collect the wet fish. I can remember serving chips to customers at Bagworth up to the age of seventeen, so I must have served my future wife, Ida Littler. Although I didn't know her then, she says she was a regular visitor to Harold's chip van.

In 1949 Harold's leg deteriorated to the extent that it had to be amputated but still he didn't give in. As soon as he came out of rehabilitation he was back in the driving seat whenever help was short. He admits that when he was hard pressed, he drove his van with only one leg - using a walking stick to work the throttle.

Eventually, the work in the chip van got the better of even his indomitable spirit, so forcing him to reluctantly sell the van, but he didn't give in - he rented a chip shop at the bottom of Gladstone Street. It was owned by Harratt's, the wood merchants. In the meantime his brother, Arthur, came home from his posting in Burma. Upon demob, Arthur was welcomed into the Talbott 'fish and chip brigade' and worked closely with Harold for a time. Our Arthur was eventually awarded a council house at Newbold Verdon and got a job at Bagworth pit to make ends meet.

I remember our ancient potato peeler. It was driven by a single cylinder petrol engine, ignited by magneto and cooled by an open water tank. You had to start it by cranking a handle and people could hear its slow pop-pop-popping for miles around. Just the thing Snibston Museum would jump at, now.

In our Overton Road home, we drew drinking water from a pump located halfway down our long garden path. It is no longer there, not even as a garden ornament. I know this because I visited the present owner, Mr Leaf, only a few months ago. He made me very welcome and I had the pleasure of roaming over my old house and grounds, a thing I had not had the opportunity to do for forty years. It was arranged by our Harold, who accompanied me on this nostalgic visit.

I noticed that several buildings had vanished but this was 1993, not 1933. No longer was the old pig sty there. The old dry loo, located at the very bottom of the garden, had been demolished. In its place was a modern garage with a modern car. That old outbuilding where Grandad kept his prize bantams was gone. Our rabbit sheds had obviously long been spirited away. The coal house used to be part of the cottage but had now been integrated into the living accommodation. The plum and apple trees I used to climb had gone. So were the mass of gooseberry and currant bushes but the house itself looked still remarkably like it always was, from th outside.

Next door is the 1480 cottage which belonged to the Swingler family for man years. Drinking water was obtained here by bucket and well. I used to watcl fascinated as Mr Swingler wound down the bucket, pausing while it filled wit. crystal clear water. He'd then drop the pawl on the ratchet wheel, wind up th. precious cargo while I stood listening to the overflow trickling off the brimmin; bucket and echoing as it fell back down the depths. I remember saying, "I wish w had a well instead of a pump - wells are much more fun." Besides, I had a fev wishes that urgently needed granting.

As my Grandad was a farm labourer at Lodge Farm in Overton Road, I was in . privileged position to roam the farmland unimpeded. The farmer, Jimmy Crane although quick-tempered and hostile at times, never restricted my urge to roam hi land. Perhaps it was because Jimmy's grandson, David Rose, who stayed with then at the Lodge often enough, was my best pal. All our spare time was spent playin; together on the farm.

At sheep dipping times David and I were always in the thick of it. On one occasio he was even more so than usual. The pond, specially constructed for shee; dipping, was adjacent to the farm - it still is today, though now dried up and fille(with debris. It used to be replenished with clean water by a natural spring. Th sheep had first to swim through a narrow lock system where the sheep di treatment fluid was added. It used to smell vile. On this day David lost his balanc and fell headlong into the mire. He seemed a long while coming to the surface and what a sight when he did! His head was completely covered in this thick, slim mud. His grandad, Jimmy Crane, went berserk. No thought of poor old David nearl drowning. He was only concerned that further sheep dipping was halted until sucl time as the muddy water had settled.

From very small, I was given many rides on the carts and hay wagons, pulled b mighty shire horses. There were no tractors at Lodge Farm in those days. Ever when they arrived nobody on the farm either wanted engine powered mechanisa tion nor had the slightest clue how to drive them. Harry Crane hated tractors anc would have nothing to do with them for years.

Two shire horses at Lodge Farm stand out in my mind. Punch was a powerfu brown shire. Captain was a black horse with white fetlocks and of great stature. M first ride on Captain was a hair-raising experience. I must have been only four year old when it happened. Grandad had put me on Captain's back and was leading hin by the halter. We reached a fastened gate and, as was usual, Grandad gave th horse his head while he opened it. Captain promptly wandered to the roadside anc lowered his head to feed on the lush grass. I'll never forget my terror, gradually slipping down his neck, trying vainly to cling to his mane. The floor is a might long way down the neck of a giant shire horse when you are pre-school age.

During the war the Home Guard used to practice doing manoeuvres up our lane. They did them at week-ends - usually Sundays. It became the usual thing to see them crawling up the hedgerows - including our garden. With blackened faces, tin hats and camouflaged uniforms, they'd be divided into two sides and wage war with the dummy hand grenades and rifle blanks. I used to stalk them to see which side won. I was often asked if I knew where the 'enemy' were hiding out. Then they crawled on their way and made me promise not to betray their position.

The few dwellings in Overton Road didn't have air raid shelters to take refuge from the bombing raids. Nobody told us what to do in an emergency. One bombing raid really did frighten me. The German planes, with the distinctive drone, came over. Suddenly, there were four high-pitched whistling bombs, falling one after the other. I put my head under the pillow but there was no hiding from the blast. They were big ones. We were bounced out of bed.

The next morning we investigated the nearby fields. We found two massive craters only two fields away, on Hawksworth's pasture. The holes were still steaming and the smell was vile. For months afterwards we were picking up small pieces of shrapnel. If I didn't know it before, I now knew there was a war on - and it had reached us! Every Sunday morning afterwards, people took their usual walk and headed for 'the craters'. It became a bizarre local landmark.

From our house, at any given time during the war, we could see several sets of barrage balloons suspended above the horizon. Grandad would say one group was over Coventry. They were protection from low-flying enemy aircraft. One Sunday morning I happened to hear on the wireless that two of the massive balloons had broken free and were drifting north. I looked outside and was astonished to see the two rogue barrage balloons in the sky. They were dragging severed steel cables, which trailed behind in a wide arc. Hardly had I got over the shock, than out of the clouds zoomed two Spitfires, banking and firing machine guns at them. Each plane shot down one balloon in a single rapid burst. Then, circling in a graceful duet, the Spitfires majestically exited. The balloons deflated and writhed like wounded elephants as they drifted earthward. I watched from the roof of our pig sty as they fell out of sight behind the hill. No doubt they were farther away than they appeared, being so large, because I didn't hear any more about them.

I loved living in the country - but it had its setbacks. Like the time when our Barbara and I happily played outside. We walked straight onto a wasps' nest under the high hedge at the side of our house. Immediately, they attacked us and followed us into the house. We were screaming hysterically, waving our arms and brushing them out of our hair but that made the wasps even more angry. For ages afterwards, we were sweeping up dead or crawling wasps. Grandma bathed our dozens of stings with blue bags and dock leaves. It's a wonder we weren't killed. It never entered our heads to go to the doctor for treatment.

Electricity wasn't in our house until after the war. Then we had lighting in only one

41

room - there were no power points for gadgets and cookers. Anyway, the owners c our tied cottage, Crane's of Lodge Farm, wouldn't have paid a large bill.

Our Harold put a small battery powered light in the pantry. It wasn't much bette than candle light but the house was draughty and candles blew out as you carrie them about. At night we had to carefully climb the stairs with a candle, keeping cupped hand round the flame to stop it blowing out. When it was gusty, we'd ge halfway up the stairs when a sudden draught would extinguish it. We'd then hav to go back down to the fireplace and re-light the candle with a home-made spil Grandad spent hours paring long thin spills from a piece of packing-case woo Before I was allowed a sharp knife, I made spills by rolling up newspaper sheet: The rest were cut into spaces for the dry loo. Nothing was wasted.

Pre-electric darkness was illuminated by paraffin lamp. The earliest model I ca remember hanging from our oak beams had a brass fuel bowl and two flat wick: We had several lamps, the wicks Grandma trimmed every Saturday afternoon as ritual. None of them threw out much light - but then she bought an Aladdin lamj from Wheatcroft's shop. It had a circular wick and, more significantly, had a mantl surrounding it which threw out a brilliant white light. I remember it boasted man candle power output.The first time we tried to use the lamp was a catastrophe Grandma fitted the new mantle and put a match to it, like it said in the instruction: Audrey wasn't expecting it to flare up. She thought the house was catching fire an blew the mantle as hard as she could. It promptly disappeared in a thousand pieces which was unfortunate because, besides being expensive, we had to wait fortnight before we could buy a replacement.

The improved lighting gave a transformation to close work, like reading an darning socks at night but draughts were still a hazard, making the flame pop an shoot up the glass chimney dangerously.

A radio was called a wireless before the war. I remember we had to have the heav accumulator charged every two to three weeks. It was like a small car battery with handle. We had a spare, so we regularly struggled all the way up Overton Road t Bott's shop on High Street, left the dud and collected the newly charge accumulator. The wireless also required a massive 120 volt dry battery that laste about a year. For good reception we also had to have an aerial wire that stretche right down to the plum tree.

When the winter snows came, we had great fun sledging down the hill from Belcher's Bar down Overton Road. Harratt's, the coffin builders on High Street made splendid sledges for half-a-crown. He made them from the off-cuts of th coffins and they afforded him a nice little earner while waiting for further funera orders. I remember three of us boys going to Harratt's one day to collect our sledge We went round the back yard and looked through a dusty window and saw a row of coffins standing upright like mummies. Now, it wouldn't have been so bad if we hadn't just seen a 'Zombie' film at the Palace Cinema . We were gone like a bullet!

Old High Street, Ibstock by Audrey Kendrick

Down the village High Street,
Shopping was a treat,
With shops galore along the way,
I wonder how folk made them pay.
Lawrence's clothes, old-fashioned but grand,
Ilty's furniture, nearly all second hand.
Wheatcroft's, where we purchased a screw to wheel-barrow,
The old tin shop, with ribbons broad and narrow.
Mr Newman, the baker of that crusty new bread,
Was a sight to delight and it's got to be said
No additives added, no polythene wrap,
Just a lovely aroma as it left the rack.
Moreton's fish, the best you could buy,
The chemist with concoctions for bad backs to a stye.
White's, the shoe shop stocked brands of renown,
Trusting folk weekly with just half-a-crown down.
Worthington's stores established to last,
Gave way to the times, now just part of the past.
Gone the starched aprons, the till with the ting,
The art of wrapping groceries in brown paper and string.
There were butchers; Jim Bailiss, Jakes Fletcher, George Newman,
Gantlet's for sweets with Collier's and Truman.
Beadall's, Bill Otty, with fruit and veg of all kind,
And Old Georgie Cornwall comes to my mind.
Eggington's papers, plugs and batteries Wilf Bott,
The Star with Morri Jones, Jordan's paints, the lot.
There was no need to travel in winter for heat,
Cos all one required was sold down High Street.

Don Gimson (tape-recording)

I was brought to Ibstock from Warwickshire at four years of age in 1905 and I wen to the National School in Grange Road. At five I was transferred to the new scho on Melbourne Road when it first opened in 1906. Mr Stevens, the headmaster, wa very strict. In fact he used the cane too much. He gave one boy six on each han then the boy swore at him. "You budder," he called him - he was short-tongued an couldn't say bugger. Mr Stevens then beat him about the legs with the cane and th boy ran home. The school bobby had to go and fetch him and make him con back to school. I was given the cane once for fidgetting. He gave me one on eac hand.

Mr Stevens played cricket for Ibstock. At school he had a block of wood made as wicket and he used to get the boys to try to bowl him. If anyone bowled him, H would give them tuppence. I can only ever remember one boy who managed t bowl him and that was Horace Woodward. He got the tuppence. Mr Stevens was good bat.

We learned sums and writing and that sort of thing. There wasn't the variety o things like there is today in schools. I was amazed when I went back to school, fc the first time, the other day, to see the variety of things they learn now. I was i Miss Tredinnick's class when I left school. One day the lesson was about farmin and the one who answered the most questions correctly would win a loaf and half pound of butter. The last question was, where does bran come from? I answere "The skin of wheat." That was it, I'd answered the the most questions and I won th prize which I took home to Mother.

We lived next door to a farm and I used to fetch the cows in, in the Summer, at fiv o'clock in the morning. On the way, I used to collect mushrooms to take to my da He loved mushroom pudding. I daren't take them up to the farm or Mr Walker, th farmer, would have taken them off me. So I used to wrap them in a handkerchi and leave them at the bottom so that I could pick them up on the way back. Foo was always short. Sometimes I would go to school with only a piece of turnip t eat.

My dad earned twenty-five shillings a week. He gave my mother a pound and sh had to manage to keep a big family. She had had seventeen children but they didr all survive. When we started to go to work, things began to improve.

My father worked very hard. He was a clay modeller and used to bring clay hom to make models. He made moulds for the big interceptors and rainwater shoes a Ellistown pipe works. The manager asked once if he could make miniatures of th products to be used as samples. He brought a lump of clay home to make th miniatures - they were to be used as ink-wells for big firms in London. He wante to make the moulds at home as he didn't want anybody to learn his secrets. He ha been taught by a Frenchman and had a set of modelling tools made out of chen wood. He also made large moulds of lions, tigers, rabbits etc. which were used as decoration for buildings. They use machines these days for such things but he made them all by hand. He also made stew pots for Mother which would boil for half an hour after they were removed from the heat.

At thirteen, I left school and started to work at Ellistown Pipe Works, under my father. One day somebody was rolling up little bits of clay and throwing them about. My father asked me who had done it and I wouldn't tell but he kept on at me about it. Because I wouldn't tell, he beat me up at home, in his temper. My mother made me leave the pipe works on account of that so I left and went to Ibstock Pit. My job was pulling a haulage rope over a twenty-four tub jig. I left and went to Ellistown but I didn't stay there long. I worked under Mr Bourne who, because I was in his choir, gave me an easy job. When I decided to leave, he put me on pony driving to serve my notice. He sent me with a horse that kicked a bit and writhed and squealed. I lockered him up - that is I put a piece of wood between the spokes of the tub to make it harder for him to pull. That made him sweat and nearly killed him off, but I tamed that horse. I think Mr Bourne did it to spite me. I was in my teens when I joined the Primitive Methodists' choir and Mr Bourne was the conductor. He was a good tenor. The lads and the girls used to put on concerts for the benefit of the chapel.

I went back to work at Ibstock pit for a shilling a week more. By then I had a wife to consider. It was a dangerous, hard job, clipping tubs onto a rope. In 1928 I broke the record on this job by clipping 1006 tubs, one at a time, in a shift of seven and a half hours. Mr Cutts, the undermanager, said, "Well done!" and gave me two shillings extra.

My wife, who was only twenty-four, died on the first day of the strike in 1926. The owners wanted to drop the wages and lengthen the day. We were on strike for six months and went back to no change. Neither the owners nor the miners would give way. My brother and I had an allotment which kept the family going during the strike. We couldn't have managed without it. I went to Gresley Common to help sink a shaft and earned £1. 3s. which I took home to Mother so that we could have a good meal. We had bread and cheese with butter. We'd been living, mainly, on potatoes, carrots and parsnips. Sometimes we had a rabbit from a poacher and we arranged to pay the one and six for the rabbit when we went back to work. At that time I was paying for an insurance policy and I told Mr Hardy, the collector, that I couldn't pay, so he paid it for me and I paid him back when we started back to work. It became due in 1928 and brought me £105, which really set me up.

I used to go boxing training and I'd always been a fighter. During the strike, my brother Owen and I fixed up a gym in Chapel Street at our dad's hairdressing shop. We had a punch ball but never told anybody. There was a youth who wanted to fight my brother and Mr Clarke, the butcher, said he would put up twenty pounds. Another chap, Sid Ball, did some sparring with my brother, but he only lasted two and a half rounds with Owen. Sid went straight to the lad who wanted the fight and told him and the lad called it off. We never got the twenty pounds. We had trained secretly, at night and my brother used to run every day, to and from Barleston where he had a hairdressing shop. I've trained hundreds of lads. I had eleven champions in sixteen years, including Dougie Ralston who won the Seven Counties Championship three times.

B Hardington

I was born on the 25 May 1911 and my first recollections are of teachers: Mr Stevens, Miss Harratt, Miss Ball, Mr F W Stevens (Headmaster), Mr Forrester (Dicky), Mr G Graver and Miss Treddinnick. Mr Stevens lived two doors away from the school and we used to scrump his apples. Magistrate Alderman Eggington lived next to the school. Mr Sykes, Sanitary Inspector for Market Bosworth Rural District Council, lived next door to Mr Stevens and rode a motor cycle and sidecar, B.S.A registration AY 2217. Always the first number to go on our list of car numbers. The next was FA 1000 which belonged to Alderman J T Jaques, who lived in High Street and was connected with the brickworks.

Parade Sunday saw the Hospital Parade around the village led by Ibstock Town Band with the United Silver Prize Band, Church Lads' Brigade, etc. and Mr Eggington, who was an official of the Fund.

The Hospital Parade

Wakes Sunday evening saw the Parish Church full and hymns accompanied by the Town Band. The Rector was the Reverend Samuel Flood, followed by the Reverend A H Birks and the Reverend M J Newbery. The Wakes amusements were in the Ram Hotel field at the rear of the Palace Cinema.

We used to go to Saturday afternoon pictures for two pennies. Shouts of "Shine!" and "Shut that door!", when the side door was opened. The weekly serial, Eddie Polo, on the silent screen ran a competition. The words NOW WATCH would flash followed, a few frames later, by WHAT DID EDDIE SAY? and everyone would shout out the words as they appeared. I never did hear of anyone winning the competition.

Herbert Moreton walking round the aisles at the interval with his basket of chocolates, etc. strapped to his shoulders and Alty Adcock playing the piano accompaniment to the pictures. A lady did this, too, but I forget her name.

Ibstock Town Cricket Club playing cricket on the Ram Field with Jock Palmer and Bert Foster bowling and Ernie Robinson, Flamsons and Adcocks batting. It was Derby Day when they played Coalville Town or Heather. Ibstock Ivanhoe played cricket on the Hastings Arms' field.

Crocodile of children marching hand in hand from the Church Sunday School along High Street to the Parish Church at 10.30 a.m. each Sunday for morning service. On one occasion we noticed R B Thirlby was advertising HOME MADE SAUSAGE in foot high white lettering on his shop window. In the afternoon we skilfully altered it to NO MAD SAUSAGE, much to everyone's amusement.

Going for long walks on Sunday afternoons, down Harrison's Yard and across the Four Leys and on towards Nailstone or Odstone. In the winter we would slide or skate on Church Hill pond.

Playing fag cards (skimming) and marbles (liney or ringy) outside Mr Green's baker's yard wall frontage. In the evenings playing 'Stag', 'Tinnalurkey', 'Kunja', and other hide and seek games in the street or front gardens. Always on the look out for Bobby Iliffe and later P S Screaton.

The advent of the Midland Red Bus caused us to run out shouting, "Red Emma!" They were so different from Fowkes', Bircher's, Rudin's, Hipwell's and Windridge buses.

Hazy recollections of Flower Shows and Sports on the Royal Oak field off Melbourne Road. There was running and cycle racing and the Milands' Green Track Cycling Championships were sometimes held there. A lot of money changed hands on the racing. It was usually Holland's Fairground Amusements, same as at the Wakes.

Buses only ran to Coalville and to Leicester (mainly for workers), so when I started at Dixie Grammar School, Market Bosworth, in 1921, I had to catch the 7.37 a.m. milk train from Heather and Ibstock to Bosworth (Loughborough to Nuneaton line) and return on the 4.20 p.m. motor train, put on specially for the schoolboys.

Going on Sunday School outings in Cherry's Brake, a horse drawn vehicle, also used for taking parties to Bagworth Station. I remember the Church Lads' Brigade marching up Common Hill to Bagworth Station en route for camp at Lytham.

My first bicycle was bought from Harry Fowkes' Cycle and Motor Cycle Shop in Chapel Street, for cycling the five miles to school at Market Bosworth. Later, in 1929, a motor cycle (Raleigh 240cc) also from Harry Fowkes for riding to work at L.M.S. Railways, Stockingford.

I played hockey for Ibstock Mixed Hockey Club from about 1928 until the war intervened. I played on Central School pitch for two years then transferred to Mr Peat's field and dressing accommodation was provided by Mrs Hardington (my mother) at 168 Melbourne Road.

For a short period I was a member of the Black Imps Concert Party an auxiliary of the Junior Imperial League (Young Tories). We rehearsed at Dr Wilson's house and were trained by a Miss Freckleton.

The Parish Church organists I remember were Mr Dunston, Walter Baxter, Harry Walker and Walter Handford who played for many years until the late Eric Elton took over. Mr Dunston, headmaster of the Church School, also supervised the Sunday School and would appear in the afternoon in time to play the piano for the closing hymn. His favourite was No: 176 'How Sweet the Name of Jesus Sounds'. It is still one of my favourites.

I was the sixth child of a family of twelve. Three children died in the 1918-1919 flu epidemic. All the rest of us reached, at least, our 70th year. I am the oldest survivor having two younger sisters aged 72 and 70 still living.

Memories of my early years by George Moore

I was born on 21st September 1915, in one of the cottages which used to stand opposite Milestone House, on Melbourne Road.

I remember my early days as a pupil at the school on Melbourne Road. I had lost my father in the flu epidemic of 1918, and had been taken in by my grandparents who lived at 29, Melbourne Road.

My early days at the junior school were the start of my schooling. I only remember two teachers - Miss Harratt, who I believe is still with us, and Miss Frederick. I remember the slate and pencil I started with, in my earliest recollections, before moving on to pencil and paper and books. We were taught the three Rs - reading writing and arithmetic, the alphabet, how to form letters and figures and how to recognise them. We learned our multiplication tables, which we had to recite and remember. We were taught how to read and how to form sentences. As we grew older, we moved up a class, where there would be further subjects taught. I was never much good at free-hand drawing, whether it was in pencil or colour.

Our school day was split into various lessons, sometimes taken by a different teacher. History and geography, the Scriptures, music, handwriting and English, which included the first essay you wrote, when you got to a certain class. I remember we were also taught how to recognise various objects to name them and to spell their names. There used to be about twenty pupils in each class. I remember at the junior school, we had forms to sit on and a narrow table to work on. I believe the school hours were 9.00am - 12 noon and 1.30pm - 3.30pm. All pupils had to go home for dinner at 12 noon and return at 1.30pm, whatever the weather. I remember games played with bean bags, inside school and, weather permitting, with balls, or skipping ropes, and various other childhood games.

Winter was the worst time for us, as we had to walk to school in all weathers, twice a day. I remember some days it would be very cold but, for the life of me, I cannot remember how the classrooms were heated. I do know that if your clothes were wet, you sat in them. If the weather was too bad, the school would let us go early in the afternoon. I remember also, the classrooms were lit, as were the streets, by gaslight.

I enjoyed my early days at the junior school, but there came a time when we had to leave it behind and go to a new school, which had been built on New Road, as we called it, which is now called Central Avenue. This was the new Ibstock Modern School, only a matter of 250 to 300 yards from the junior school. I believe I moved to this school either in late 1925 or early 1926. This was a complete change from the school I had just left. It had large, airy classrooms and a large main hall where we had morning assembly. This was a mixed school of boys and girls and was built in the shape of a rectangle with two sets of classrooms running along both long sides, divided by the big hall. There were two entrances, one for boys and one for the girls. Each had a large cloakroom at the entrance. Each wing had its own playground which were towards High Street and divided down the middle by an iron fence. There was also a large playing field which ran from the school building to the boundary of the jitty. Just inside the field from the jitty stood the science, woodwork and metalwork classroom, which meant that when you attended these lessons, you had to walk from the school to the science centre, across the playing field.

Mr J V Measures was the headmaster who, until his death in a car accident, was a man of great stature, as far as Ibstock was concerned. He was a kindly man but a strict disciplinary headmaster. The school was where you were prepared, by your own efforts, for the outside world, into which you were introduced at the ripe old age of 14. It was where I was taught maths, English, geography, science and history. These for me were my favourite subjects. I was good at maths, but for the life of me I could not master algebra. I was also good at the other subjects, but my favourite subject was English, especially essays and hand-writing. Sport was also one of the things we were encouraged to take up. The school, both boys and girls were split into four houses - Arden (yellow), Cranbourne (red), Charnwood (green) and Sherwood (blue). A yearly sports day was held, with all four houses competing for the school trophy. Also, individual winners of all other events were held. Sports day was a big day to look forward to. Many Ibstock people used to turn up for this event.

Your education started from where you left off at the Junior School, but with one big exception - here you were taught, apart from your lessons, discipline and civility. Even outside school, during school times, if you met your teacher on the street, you were expected to call him Sir. This was also a strict rule inside school. remember one teacher, and I believe all the old pupils of this period will not forget him, who some of us were very wary of. His name was 'Daddy' Wright. He was, so they said, a South African. His idea of discipline was to throw the blackboard scrubber at you, if you upset him. If you lifted the lid of your desk up to miss it you probably finished up with a cuff around the ear. But he was, to me, a good teacher, as far as his job was concerned. One teacher I can remember was Dicki Wells. He was the science master, and his lessons, to me, were always interesting. The woodwork and metalwork teacher was Mr Sabine. He was a master craftsman at his job, but I invariably finished up with something out of a fairy story. Another teacher I remember was Ant Harris, the sports master. He also ran the school football team, which was a member of the Coalville and District Schools League. will always remember the first time I was picked to play for the school team, in 1928, towards the end of the season. I played with the team until I left school in 1929.

A school Christmas party was held at the school and each pupil was given a Christmas present. Just before Christmas, entertainment was provided and staff used to join in. The best party, as far as I was concerned, was the one when I left school in December 1929. When school broke up for the Christmas break, Mr Measure wished me and my friends who left at the same time, a happy future, and gave us a handshake to take into a completely new world.

Although my school days were, to me, happy days, the happiest days were when we were not at school, especially during the light days. Then we used to get together, boys and girls, to play games; tin-tin-a-lurkie, marbles, whip and top, duck stones, faggies, bowling hoops, snobs and humpty dumpty. But the best days were when we used to 'gang up' and roam around the country pathways. During the early Spring, we used to go bird-nesting, and used to think nothing, at the age of ten years and upwards, of roaming as far as Shackerstone, Normanton, Nailstone and Odstone, in fact, anywhere a path would take us. The same used to apply when we went conkering and collecting blackberries and crab apples, in the Autumn. But our favourite roaming ground was the Fricklings. This was the path from Hinckley Road at the Stumps, that used to take us to Johnson's Farm. But

50

nstead of the farm path, we used to turn onto the path that took us over the railway bridge at Heather, just topside the brickyard. This led us either to the Duck Paddle at Heather, or across to the pond where we used to collect frog spawn, or played around, before going under the railway bridge that led to the Bannies where, in the Summer months, we used to paddle and bathe.

Before this period, when I was allowed to play with my mates, I remember the walks I used to go with my grandfather, with whom I used to live, if he was not at work that night. On light evenings, in the Summer at weekends, he would take me for a walk, mostly up Belcher's Bar, passing the semi-circular yard where the old Swan pub used to stand, with I believe two cottages and stables. We used to cut across from the Swan, along Smith's footpath, which was opposite the pub. This used to bring us out nearly opposite Grassy Lane, which led us to Barton-in-the-Beans. My grandfather was friendly with the Didecoys who used to camp on the side of the brook which crossed the pathway. He sometimes used to stop and talk to them, whilst enjoying his pipe. These were the gypsies who used to come round selling peppermint and clothes pegs. We used to stop at the Swan occasionally, but I believe it was knocked down while I was very young.

On dark evenings, after I had done my homework, I was allowed out for an hour or so but always had to be in by eight o'clock. One of the games we played then was window tapping. This consisted of a button on a piece of cotton, which you used to sneak up and fix with a drawing pin on to the window frame. This was done when it was a bit windy. Another game was spout roaring, which was the most tricky. Paper was stuffed up the bottom of the down-pipe that used to carry the water off the roof, and set the paper alight. It used to create a hell of a roar, and you had to be quick to get away, or else you were likely to get a good hiding.

My two aunts were devout Methodists. Aunt Doll used to play the piano and my other aunt used to play the violin. My grandfather worked on the night shift as a holer. I never saw him work on day shift. He used to walk it to Nailstone Pit and back, every time he had to go to work. Owing to my aunt, I had to attend the Methodist Chapel regularly. Morning, afternoon and evening on a Sunday, and Band of Hope, Bible Reading and Scriptures during the week. They also used to hold Temperance Evenings. I know I did not like it, but I must admit, it taught me how to write, read and spell, a fact which showed in my school work.

Electricity had been brought into Ibstock. The streets were bright at night, but the most marked event was the installation of electric lighting in the houses. No. 29 had electricity installed in the middle of the 1920s, and I remember what a difference it made, when you no longer had to rely on a paraffin lamp and candles, and found it a lot easier to do your homework and chores. These jobs consisted of fetching drinking water from the row's community pump. The causey was very uneven, and you certainly had to watch where you put your feet. The soft water (rain water) was stored in an underground sump, under the kitchen, at the side of a porch. You used to draw your washing-up water from this by means of a small pump on the side of a stone sink. This was called the wash-house. It also contained a large copper set over a fire grate, which used to be lit on wash-days and bath-days. Bath night for me was Saturday, when I used to bath in a large tin bath filled up with hot water from the copper. During winter nights on these bath-days, you always made sure you had a good fire under the copper.

At about the age of twelve years, I took up fishing. My uncle, Wag Parry, used to take me down to the fish pond at the rear of the church. I spent many happy hours down there. I then started to go fishing with Jackie Storer, Bendy Bailey and Tommy Storer on some Saturday mornings. We used to go by train from Heather Station, complete with fishing tackle and snap. I believe the train used to run at 8am in the morning to Shackerstone Canal. The return was at 6pm. The fare was, for me, fourpence return. The favourite spot for Bendy and Co. was the Monthills, which was in between the first bridge over the canal from Ibstock, and the bridge near the Rising Sun pub. It did not matter if you did not catch anything, there was always another Saturday, and you had enjoyed yourself on the canal bank.

One Man's Ibstock by Harold Talbott

I was born May 8th 1920. I was just a six-year-old boy when I left Nailstone with my parents, Mr William and Mrs Emily Talbott, and came to live in Overton Road, Ibstock. I remember our furniture piled high on the horse-drawn dray, as we did our own furniture removing. It was a slow, bumpy job, Dad driving the horse along the pot-hole ridden road with all our worldly goods piled high. My brothers and sisters also made the journey. The youngest, Barbara, was yet to be born.

Dad worked for Jimmie Crane on his farm at Nailstone. When Jimmie moved, in 1926, to Lodge Farm in Overton Road, Ibstock, Dad moved also. I think the farm was actually owned by Pagets, and Cranes had a lease. It was the start of a new life for all of us. Here, we grew up through our schooldays, until the traumas of war saw the family split up. Dad stayed on in this cottage until his retirement in 1954, aged 68, when he was forced to move.

One strange, regular incident of the 1930s was rather eerie to me, as a youngster. A horse-drawn vehicle carrying a large tank used to call at our house in the middle of the night, about 2am, and men would empty the dry toilet pan into this tank. Later, the vehicle was motorised. Before that period, Dad buried everything at the bottom of the garden. Some folks' lavatories were two-seaters - just a wide board with two appropriate holes side-by-side to sit on.

I remember, as a schoolboy, an eccentric shopkeeper at 4 High Street, opposite the Palace Cinema. The old buildings are all gone now. His name was George Cornwall. He sold sweets, among other things, and he used to frighten all the kids to death. He had cats and they used to lie all over the sweets in the window. He'd move a cat to serve you and there'd be cat hairs all over them. He was a real character.

Peggy Andrews, whom I later married, was in the Red Garries Carnival Band which flourished before the war. The large Andrews family lived at 2 Church View. Some of Peggy's sisters were in the band, too. Peggy Mee was an accordionist, whose father, Arthur Mee, ran the Red Garries. My wife twirled the baton and later played the accordion on the march. The baton twirling leader was Phyllis Ball, who greatly impressed the crowds by her skill, throwing her stick as high as the houses, catching it on the march with an aptitude worthy of a Chinese juggler. She was brilliant. The last time I heard, she was living at Ellistown. These parades of the 30s were always led by about four riders on horseback. I played the accordion in the Rainbow Band. Peggy still has her accordion and she won't part with it for any money. It's a sort of heirloom. I also played the harmonica quite a lot. It was easy to carry around - instant entertainment!

The Red Garries

George Nicholls who unfortunately died prematurely, was my best mate. He was related to the Nicholls family who kept the general grocery shop at the bottom of Reform Road.

I was saddened to learn of the death of Neddie Towers. Neddie was a distinctive character of the village who entertained at many functions. He had a voice just like Gracie Fields and always wore immaculate make-up for his performances. There couldn't have been one person in Ibstock who did not know of Neddie. He lived down Harrison's Yard. You had to dive off the High Street under an archway to reach it. We regularly used Harrison's Yard as a short cut across the fields to our home in Overton Road.

The Toc H was located up Reform Road, the narrow lane by the side of Nicholls' shop. Talbot House was another name for Toc H, a coincidence since Talbott is my name. We used to go to Toc H every week. It was a social hall, catering for a variety of functions for working people. Peggy practised there with the Red Garries.

Peggy and I lived in Double Row when first married, in 1943. We were married in St Denys' Church by the Rev Newbery, who used to bellow out his sermons with such force you never forgot them. Our first home was one room, halfway up Gladstone Street (Deakin's Lane). The Double Row is all gone now. It was set back from the road and ran at right angles to it. We lived with Peggy's grandma, across from the Boot public house. Later, the Council gave us a prefabricated house on Sunnyside estate, off Church View.

I had my leg off in 1949 while serving with the RAF. The top RAF doctor of that day, Sir Stamford Cade, told me I'd never walk again. I wrote to the hospital in 1993 and assured them I could walk and had even ridden a bicycle with one leg from Ibstock to Market Bosworth, daily, - a distance of six miles each way. We had a lovely letter and a card back from the hospital in acknowledgement, which arrived on our recent Golden Wedding anniversary.

After a posting to South Africa, I was sent back on a hospital ship in 1943. For my last couple of years' service, I was stationed at Blaby. Whenever a plane came down, it was our job to recover it. We'd take off the wings, tail section, etc. and load them onto our huge transporter lorry, called a Queen Mary. They were the longest vehicles on the road in those days. One large plane came down at Odstone, near a farmhouse. It was only about two miles from my home in Overton Road. I would have loved to have slipped home for a cup of tea and a hot meal. Another plane came down between Belcher's Bar and Nailstone Wood pit. Of all the planes I helped recover, none were German. They were either British or American. There were 13 gangs of us working, mostly in the Northampton, Coventry and Peterborough areas.

One flying machine I shall always remember was the R101 airship. I'd be about eleven at the time in the early 1930s. It flew over Ibstock when I was at Junior School. The teachers let us out so that we could watch it. It was massive and could be seen for miles.

Because my father's house was a tied cottage, Jimmie Crane expected us children to perform certain farm duties on Saturday mornings. One regular job I had to do was to clean out the hen houses. Other jobs were trimming lawns, weeding flower borders and picking damsons and apples for storage. For that sort of work I'd get about a shilling. Mrs Crane originally came from Huddersfield, a coincidence, since my mum originated from Huddersfield. She was called Kilburn before becoming a Talbott.

Hubert Bircher ran the motor omnibus company on the High Street in the early 1930s. It later became Bircher Brothers, haulage contractors. At least one of their lorries had detachable seats. They could deliver loads of freight, then convert the lorry into public transport by adding seats. Their mechanic, Bertie Lamb, was a character. He used to have more oil on his jacket than in the lorries. His clothes absolutely shone with oil. He would go straight from work to the Whimsey Inn for a pint of ale. He was only a little chap - just right for crawling under lorries and tight spaces!

Walter Mears' blacksmith's shop at 115 High Street was a place I visited for hours at a time when I came from school. So fascinated was I by his work, that I used to stop and help him. I also went with Dad, taking the farm horses for shoeing, and carts for repair. One of my favourite jobs was pumping the hand-bellows while he worked at the forge. Besides shoeing horses, he used to sharpen local miners' tools. Peggy's dad, Bert Andrews, regularly had his pick heads sharpened by him. They were detached from the wooden shafts by knocking out a small steel wedge. Walter would heat the pick heads in his forge and draw the points by hammer and anvil. He then tempered and case-hardened the tips. Another blacksmithing job was making long wedges, the miners using them for splitting huge lumps of coal at the coalface. Mr Andrews finished his time at Bagworth mine. After an injury, he was made gateman at a clay hole in Bagworth.

My dad worked at Ibstock pit for a time. It seems there was a lot of water in the workings. On one occasion, he and other miners had to go running for their lives when water gushed out. After an injury sustained at the pit, Dad left to do farm work. He wasn't a miner for very long.

Our doctor was Dr Meldrum, but there was another doctor who used to visit us, at one time, who had the amazing habit of sitting on our fire-guard and eating hot potatoes straight from our saucepan. Then there was Dr Agnew who was a medical officer of health and public vaccinator. He had something to do with the isolation hospital, which was situated about two fields across from the cemetery. It's a pig farm now, I believe.

I can remember David Manton, the plumber. Manton's Corner on High Street is named after his family. He had a tiny shop front and in the window he always put a toilet on display. That blessed toilet was there for years and years along with the same roll of wallpaper and a tin of whitewash. An important character was John Thomas Jacques. He was a JP whose private residence was called The Motts, which later became the British Legion Club on High Street. Then there was J Lawrence and Sons, on Melbourne Road who were printers. Jim Satchwell was projectionist at the Palace picture house. Mr Baker had a fruit and vegetable shop in Chapel Street. He used to come round, selling his wares, with a horse and dray. It may have been a nickname, but we school kids called the town crier, 'Dickie Pepper'.

At the top of Crown Hill, just inside Melbourne Road, was the Town Hall and Fire Station. They had a hand-pulled fire engine in those days. Later, they pulled it with horses which grazed off Station Road. The band used to practise halfway up Crown Hill on the right hand side. The Swifts football team used to play behind the Royal Oak, on Melbourne Road.

We used to have a milkman named Osbourne who came from Barton-in-the-Beans. He had a horse-drawn float, originally, but later had a motorised vehicle. There were no milk bottles then - he used to measure out the milk straight from a churn and tip it into the customer's jug. I used to ride with him, as kids do. But on one occasion, I let his brake off and the float ran away with me.

In 1947, we were snowed under and all the workers had to go on the dole for two weeks. We couldn't get through to factories at Earl Shilton and Barwell for the snowdrifts. In places, the drifts were double-decker height. The works' bus took us each morning to where we'd dug the day before and we'd start digging again. It took us a full fortnight to get the bus through. Virtually all the villagers had to join in the great dig. Coal merchants couldn't deliver and bakers couldn't distribute bread. Mee's, the Ibstock baker, made deliveries, house to house, by sledge.

Dad had to fetch coal with a horse-drawn cart, in the old days, from Nailstone Wood pit. He also made regular visits, taking farm milk, in churns, to Bagworth railway station. I was able to ride with him on Sundays. I remember, from my earliest youth, the miners walking across the fields to Bagworth and Nailstone pits. There was no transport available then, so they had to walk it, every shift. During the great strike of 1926, local lads took their fathers' cross-cut saws and went logging in the fields. My brothers and I joined them, sawing suitable branches off any trees we could. That was, until the local policeman caught us and smacked us around the ear-holes. The burly man confiscated our dad's saw and Dad had to go, that night, to the policeman's house and ask for it back. Then we got another clip round the ear when he got us home.

At school, we had to be extra polite to the teachers and we had to tip our caps to them and call them Sir or Miss. We were frightened to death of them.

One of the main highlights of the year was the Co-op treat. All the members' children were eligible to attend. I think we met at Coalville or Ravenstone in a large field. Everybody from all around met on this great day out. We walked from Ibstock in a trailing line to the meeting point. We were each given a bag containing crisps and an apple for our tea. There were sports events to watch and participate in.

Almost everyone was in the Co-op. Mam would write out all the week's provisions she needed in a book provided by the Co-operative Society. We then took our book to the shop where the assistants neatly wrapped up the order with brown paper and string. They'd then make a weekly delivery to our door. Goods were not pre-packed, then - sugar, butter, etc. had to be weighed out from bulk. The shop assistant would take your money, place it in a canister and put that in a long suction pipe, leading to the cashiers. We had to wait until they blew back the canister with our change and receipt.

Dad always kept a sheepdog to accompany him on the farm. One of the better known ones was called Jess. She had a lot of puppies during her long life. Dad used to train them and then sell them for a few pints of ale.

Elsie Gibson (tape-recording)

I was born in Spring Cottages, in Ibstock, in 1925. When my older sister, Violet, was born in 1914, my parents got one of the four cottages down the Spring Road. After my father came back from the Great War, he went to work at Ibstock Brick and Pipe where he made seals for joining the pipes. The seals were made from material similar to pitch which gave off fumes and a lot of heat and this gradually burned my father's eyes so that eventually he went blind. I used to love to go and watch him work. He had a little cabin at the back of the brickyard. There were no fork-lifts in those days, only ponies to pull the loaded trolleys. My father would carry a load of pipes, four high, from the kilns to the lorries. Women worked there on the loading and everything was done manually. My dad got a medal for working 50 years in the clay industry.

In the Spring Cottages there was no tap water, pump water, gas or electricity. We had a copper and a little boiler at the side of the black-leaded grate for hot water. All the cooking was done in the oven at the side of the fireplace, where my mother kept big, white enamel buckets, filled with spring water. My father had put a pipe into the wall of the brook for the clear spring water to flow through. That was what we drank. It was as clear as crystal and even in the coldest weather it never froze because it flowed from out of the earth. It was lovely. We all used to like paddling in the brook but never went barefoot because of the blood-suckers. One day when I was a toddler, my mother had got me dressed in clean clothes and put my sister Violet in charge of me. One of the other children dared Violet to jump the brook. She went to jump, I grabbed her skirt and we both fell in. Violet managed to stop me being carried away under the bridge. We went home and got clean clothes on. Mam said, "Don't you dare go in that brook again!" Childlike, I did go in again. Violet took me home and we both got a good hiding. This time, Mother said, "I'm changing your clothes, but you're not going out. You're not going out again." I cried and cried as I wanted to play with our Violet, Bill, Joe and all the other children. At about three o'clock clouds began to build up for a thunder storm and all the kids came inside. Our Bill decided to paste things into his scrapbook and I leaned over the table to see what he was doing. He shoved me and I stepped back and sat in the bucket at the side of the fireplace. My mam said, "I've kept you in all afternoon and now you're wet through in home." She couldn't help but laugh. She kept me dry and I'd still found water.

My mother became friendly with a lady who lived two doors away from us and she invited Mother to go to the Salvation Army. That is how she came to join. My older brother and sister had to go as well. I was only a baby at the time. When they had the open air meetings with the girls playing tambourines, my brother, Joe, who was only nine, played the cornet beautifully. The bandmaster taught him. If lads wanted to join, they were found an instrument and taught to play. They played things like Onward Christian Soldiers - something you could clap to. As I got older I loved it. Church seemed so solemn and sacred but in the Salvation Army you sing and shout "Allelujah!" and it made you feel good.

Many people went to the Salvation Army at that time but when the war broke out, a lot of the little corps, like Ibstock, broke up because the officers were needed abroad. I don't think they went to fight but they went with the soldiers.

On Sunday, it was 'stick to the rules'. No toys or games. You had your bath on Saturday night and on Sunday dressed in your Sunday clothes. Like a lot of people, Mum was not very well off so she would make our dresses out of calico with a bit of broderie anglaise or lace to make them a bit different. When you'd put your clean clothes on, you daren't move. We went to the Salvation Army in the morning and the afternoon. When I first went there was a large tray, filled with building sand, with a mirror for the water in an oasis and small toy trees. The teachers brought toy people and the Bible stories were illustrated that way. They really went to town for the little ones. At six or seven, we moved up to the next Bible Class, where we read passages out, in turn. The girls were called Sunbeams. I remember my brothers wanting to and play elsewhere but we had no option. We always went and when we got there, we always enjoyed it.

At school the other children made fun of the ones who went to the 'Sally Army'. It tempted us, sometimes, to be like them. We used to think it would be nice to go and play football but my mother wouldn't let us. She'd say, "This is the Lord's day and it stays that way. You've got six other days in the week to play and do what you like."

What we liked about the Salvation Army was that it didn't matter what denomination you were, you were welcome. When the children came up to the Welfare to play on the swings, they could come in if they wanted. They would be charged a penny for a pot of peas and a noggin of bread. Mrs Troth used to get the children to recite and sing, or we played spin the bottle and paid forfeits. Dozens of children used to come.

We went to De Montfort Hall in Leicester to take part in a show with other corps. It was a series of tableaux, illustrating scenes from the Bible. One of them was the story of the wise and foolish virgins. Miss Spencer, who took the Bible class, stood at the side reading the stories. Instead of stopping while the costumes and the scenery were changed, she carried on reading, so that she'd nearly finished by the time we got the second tableau ready. It was chaotic but it got a good laugh. My Mam almost broke her heart because she was playing a foolish virgin. She cried and said, "I'm not playing that any more. I wanted to be a wise virgin and go through the door, not one that gets locked out." She really took things to heart.

When we first moved from the Spring Cottages to this house in Leicester Road, my mother was very upset. All the furniture from the cottage fitted into one room here. She hadn't got anything to go in the front room. She was so upset that she said to my dad, "Oh, Joe, let's go back."

All the other houses in Leicester Road had railings and gates but there was a wide opening at the side of ours so that the coal could be delivered to the backs of the houses. Mrs Harris, from next door, and my mam asked the Council to put up a fence at the front to keep the children off the road. Two carpenters came to do the job. The men arrived with all the materials on a large handcart. They built the fences and put a gate in the middle. When they went to go, they realised they'd shut the handcart in as it was to big too go through the new gate. They had to get someone to help them lift the cart over the fence.

I loved the Spring Cottages. There was no traffic down there and, in summertime it was lovely beside the water. We used to go fishing for sticklebacks. There was only one thing I didn't like and that was the toilets. There were two for the four houses and they were right up the top of the gardens. They were pan lavatories and we shared ours with the Windram family. I remember one time that the pans had not been emptied for some while. The cart (they used to call it the 'Violet cart'), hadn't been, so Mr Windram said he would do it. He said we couldn't live among that lot. He dug a big hole at the top of the garden, emptied the pans in to the hole and buried it. Later on, the lads, our Joe and Georgie Windram, who played together, fell out over something. Joe gave George a clout and he went crying to his mam and dad. Mr Windram came out, our Joe ran off up the garden, Mr Windram chased him and fell up to his waist in the hole where he'd emptied the pans. He'd forgotten where he'd put it.

The cottages are still there in Spring Road but they have been modernised and two houses have been made from the original four.

An Ibstock Childhood from 1928 by Horace Crane

I was born at Poplar Farm, in High Street. My father was Arch Crane; members of his family had kept the Crown Inn for over 70 years. Mother's parents, Mr and Mrs Robert Adcock, kept the Waggon and Horses. I attended Grange Road Infants School (long since closed), then Melbourne Road Junior School, headmaster Mr H Harratt, afterwards going to the Senior School in Central Avenue, where the headmaster was Mr Measures.

I remember while at Senior School assisting the woodwork teacher, Mr Sabine, in making the blackout shutters for the school windows in 1939, around the time of the outbreak of war. At that time, the school took a block of allotments for pupils to participate in the 'Dig for Victory' campaign. We also made a tool shed in the woodwork centre, then erected it for use on the allotment. All this provided a little light relief from lessons in the classroom.

Before going to school I helped deliver the milk. My father had a milk round and delivered with a pony and float. Milk was carried in large churns, a pint measure was used, then delivered to the door in special carrying cans where the householder usually had a jug waiting for the milk to be tipped into. At that time, many milk producers had small delivery rounds in the village. I recall the following: J Osborne, M Harding, H Dunnicliffe, A Ludleam, The Dawson family, T and L Redshaw, W Newman, W Hardy, G Jarvis, A Foster, W Widdowson, as well as the Co-op Dairy and others.

Many amusing incidents happened on the milk round in those days, some repeatable, some not. One concerned a well known Ibstock character of those times, a man named Harry Johnson usually called Banty. He lived on Hinckley Road and chopped firewood for a living at Enoch Cramp's woodyard in Chapel Street. Banty was a small man and extremely bowlegged. One day, when delivering the milk, my father walked round the corner of the house to be confronted by the sight of Banty, sitting on the privy seat with the door wide open. His dog sat by his side (as such old lavatory seats allowed). He was heard to say, "Fido, Fido, this day wilt thou be in paradise with me, me duckie."

Also on Hinckley Road lived three sisters, the Misses Wilkins, who made their living by hand knitting of high quality, mainly baby garments. These were collected by Wood and Johnson, carriers of Melbourne Road and taken into Leicester. Next to them lived Mort Wilkins, the cobbler.

On the second Sunday of each July the Church Parade took place, at one time quite a large affair. The procession was led by a band of men and boys on horseback. I remember taking part in this, riding the milk pony. We would all be clad in different coloured smocks and hats (the earliest arrivals getting the best outfits). Many bands took part plus the British Legion, Scouts and Girl Guides, etc. The collections went to the Royal Infirmary. I remember it amounted to over £250 one year which in those days would be quite a sizeable amount.

Now for a walk up High Street turning in from the A447 road. The parish church of St Denys stands on the corner, approached through its lovely avenue of lime trees, still as beautiful today. The Rector in those days was the Reverend Burke. The Rectory of that time being a much larger building, part of it was taken down and then divided into two separate houses. What is now the Church Hall was then the stables and coach house to the Rectory. On the wall of these buildings, by the roadside, was a notice, which read, 'Beware Spring Guns on these Premises' (surely an early form of burglar deterrent).

Cross over the top of Overton Road with the walled gardens of the Manor House coming up to the corner. Doctor Wilson lived, and had his surgery, there. Later came Doctor Meldrum, who was a very keen gardener, specialising in roses. He used to exhibit and win with them at the Chelsea Flower Show. Mr Bloomfield was his gardener. Mr D Manton, who was a painter, decorator and plumber, lived on the corner and next door lived Frank Nichols, who was the locomotive driver at Ibstock Colliery. Then came number 141, Poplar Farm, where I was born. Mr Joe Lockton, a school attendance officer, lived on the other side of the farm.

A little further up was Truman's Clothing Shop. By there and under the archway, just into South Road, lived Neddy Towers who played the piano and sang around the pubs, usually dressing as a woman, sometimes impersonating Gracie Fields. One night on a bus trip to Ashby Statutes Fair, Neddy went in full dress and played the piano at one of the pubs there. Neddy's night out nearly ended in disaster when a group of sailors who were there took a fancy to him. They kept treating him to drinks and, in the end, he had to beat a hasty retreat into the ladies' toilets and get some women to smuggle him off the premises.

The next shop on High Street was Dick Thirlby's, a high class grocery shop. Next was Len Mears - blacksmiths where I used to take the horses to be shod. Then came Doctor Agnew's house and surgery. Where Godfrey's butchers shop is now consisted of two smaller shops. The first was Miss Knight, the milliner and the other was Newman's butchers. Then it was Brown's boots and shoes. Next was Gantlet's, provisions and sweets and then Ottey's, fruit and vegetables. What is now Page's clock and watch shop was also two separate shops, Owen's, the saddlers and Tommy Smith's barber's shop. After that came Beardall's greengrocers, King's boots and shoes, Fletcher's sweet shop adjoining Fletcher's butchery, wilf Bott's hardware shop and Baylis butchers with adjoining provisions shop.

Then came the old school building on the corner of Grange Road. Here Madam Thirlby's dancing classes were held on Monday nights, where children went for tap dancing from 5.00 p.m. until 7.30 p.m. followed by ballroom dancing classes from 8.00 p.m., price one shilling. Whist drives and concerts were regularly held there. Jimmy Wallace, the school master, used to run gym classes there twice a week. Down in the bottom of Grange Road lived Dickie Gray the Town Crier. He would walk around the village ringing his bell and calling notice of meetings and social events.

Continuing along the same side of High Street came Steel's paint and decorating shop, next was Brook's clothing, Shuttleworth's menswear, Jordan's electrical and plumbing, Cramp's tobacconist followed by Cramp's footwear. Then came The Star Supply Stores and Tea Company, on the corner of Orchard Street. Across was Brownlow's chemist and general goods, Wheatcroft's ironmongers, a dress shop, then next came Harris's sweet shop, then The Ram public house kept by Mr Sammy Underwood. Next we arrive at the old Palace Picture House, then on to Moreton's fish and chip shop, Collier's sweet shop then Alty Adcock's, furniture dealer.

Alty Adcock with his Champion Racing Pigeon and John Snagge

Uncle Alty was a keen pigeon fancier, winning many prizes and trophies in races. He also played the piano at the Palace for the old silent films. Then Mee's bakery on the corner, and at the bottom of Chapel Street and junction was Curzon Street. Flour was delivered to the bakery from Sheepy Mills by an old steam lorry which could be heard approaching for quite a distance.

In Chapel Street lived Mr Hodgkin, a tailor, who used to travel around the district on foot, with his case and, invariably, accompanied by his Dalmatian dog.

Just across the road was my Uncle Walter Adcock's bakery and shop. Higher up was Harry Fowkes' garage, which used to run a bus service into Leicester. One of his drivers was Mr Bill Jacques who still talks of those days and even remembers the bus timetables. In Curzon Street stood the old gasworks, long since gone and bungalows built on the ground. Also on Curzon Street was the Waggon and Horses where my mother was born.

Now to return down the other side of High Street. There was Cyril Greasley, fruit and vegetables. Next was Georgie Cornwall's sweets and provisions, where mice scampered among goods displayed in the window. Lawrence's menswear, then came Bill Riley's shoe shop and cobbler's, Badcock's pottery shop, Crane's butchers, Hurst's vegetable shop. Harratt's house came next with yard and workshops. They were undertakers, wheelwrights and farriers. There was Jimmy Burchall's sweet shop then came a row of houses with Norman Dunnicliffe's barbers in one of the front rooms. Carrying along was Jackson's fruit and vegetables, they also went round the village selling from a horse and dray. On to Reg Chaplin's fish and chips then Mattley's general shop followed by Allen's newsagents, Alsop's butchers, G Smith's off licence, Preston's butchers and further down was Richardson's drapery with the entrance to Newman's Farm up the side. Then came a small corrugated zinc building which went under the name of Newman's Tin Shop, where knitting wools, etc. were sold.

Up the steps at the next house was a room used as the local branch of the Midland Bank. After that was Worthington's foodstore. Above the shop was a billiard hall run by Ted Black of the Whimsey Inn. Also in the same building was a room where the Ibstock British Legion held their first meetings. Next came a garage building that a haulage business had used at one time. I remember it being converted into a boxing hall. I recall boxers coming from a wide area to compete there. Local boxers were Sim Woolley, 'Snatch' Birchall and Arthur Hooton whose father was the trainer. Wilf Bott was the timekeeper and George Brown was referee.

Next stands the Whimsey Inn. Cross over the bottom of Gladstone Street where the car park now is and on the corner was George Smith's. He sold the best fish and chips. The chips there had to be cooked to perfection and served just right. When opposition opened up nearby, someone remarked they would need to move a bit faster to keep the custom. George replied, "I've seen them come and I've seen them go and I'll still be here." I enjoyed my pennyworth of chips from there quite regularly. Next came Eggington's Newsagent, Harold Newman, baker and confectioner who delivered with a horse-drawn van. Then came Turner's the butchers. Mr and Mrs Ford kept the Post Office. Then there was the garage where Bircher's buses operated from. They sold out to the Midland Red Bus Co. and turned over to haulage, carting bricks down to London and returning with fruit and veg. to Birmingham Wholesale Market.

We then come to Frank Holmes' house and orchard where I have to admit I joined my pals in a little scrumping. The rates had to be paid to Mr Holmes. Next where the new surgery now stands there lived two sisters, the Misses Ison who, by themselves, worked a coal delivery round, fetching loads of coal from the colliery with their horse and dray. Arthur Nicholl's general shop was next. Then came Baxter's Builders at Holmesdale Manor which is now the nursery school. Round the S bend is The White House - the Everitts lived there. Up the driveway alongside was Widdowson's farm. On the other side of the drive was the gardener's cottage belonging to the Manor House across the street. Bob Stafford had the carpenter's and undertaker's business at the back of there.

Cross the bottom of Hall Lane. Several cottages stood there and we reach the Crown Inn at the junction with the A447 road. At that time the landlord of the Crown was William Crane, my uncle. My sister and her husband became landlords for quite a number of years after that.

Scarlet fever and diphtheria being commonplace ailments in those days, there were two small isolation hospitals on the outskirts of the village. One was where Gimson's pig farm is now and the other was at Foster's, Blackberry Lane Farm. There are so many other things I could tell about old Ibstock but it would take far too long, it would seem to go on forever.

My Special Corner of Ibstock by Frank Gregory

I was born on Melbourne Road in 1931 but was too young to know my own Mother before she died. Yet, I lived a happy life when my Grandparents brought me up from a baby. I was treated like the youngest of their large family of eight surviving children, my aunts and uncles acting as brothers and sisters. The 'happy but poor' Talbott family of the '30s and '40s was headed by William and Emily. At intervals a chick would leave the nest to be married amid emotions of joy and sadness.

We lived at the village edge, in a cottage enchanted by nature. My youngest aunt, Barbara Talbott, was but three years older than me, so it was easy to tag on as one of the family. We were so close knit I found it impossible to call them Aunt or Uncle and, of course, as a baby I wouldn't know they were a generation removed. I affectionately referred to them as 'our Barbara', 'our Audrey' or 'our Harold', etc. as befitting any brother or sister. Here I flourished, watching them fly away one by one. Then one day marriage finally saw me also leaving the fold. My Grandparents had now become Darby and Joan.

Our lane was called Locker's Lane, alias Lover's Lane, alias Overton Road - it answered to all three and I loved it dearly. My earliest recollections go back to the early '30s. Locals know, Overton Road smacks of the 15th century with its 1480 cottage on the hill, which was home to the Swingler family in my youth. Our red bricked dwelling still stands next door and was a tied cottage to the nearby Lodge Farm, where my Grandfather toiled as farm labourer. Across the road was a small cottage inhabited by the Milward family, since demolished for a modern bungalow.

The lane starts near the church, crosses two brooks and ends at Belcher's Bar, the one-time Toll Bar. As yet unspoiled, it hosts a profusion of wildlife and flora. The disease I call 'dreaded builders' malady' has not yet struck. I know because whenever I return, some irresistible force drags me from the main road into this time warp of my youth.

The brook nearest Lodge Farm is an open ford with raised planks for walkers. This crude bridge was much higher, narrower and treacherously slippery in the old days, the brook much wider. Yet cyclists sometimes rode over. Occasionally, they paid the price - I was one! With three dozen fresh farm eggs hooked on my handlebars - intended for a wedding cake - I wobbled over the unprotected edge of planks, crashing headlong with my cycle into the bubbling water.

I squelched home and presented the soaking bag of eggs to Grandma and announced optimistically, "I don't think I've broken many." To my dismay, and downfall, there were only two eggs left intact. I tried to soften the blow somewhat by returning to the brook to pick lush watercress for tea - but Grandma wasn't swallowing that!

My earliest memories of home embrace long, warm summers. Of daylight that never seemed to turn to darkness. Of vibrant laughter drifting on the breeze from Milward's old cottage on a tranquil Sunday evening. Of the Wall's ice-cream man leisurely cycling up the long drag on his funny tricycle with the ice tub mounted in front of him. We loved best his long, three cornered fruit flavoured ices that came in all colours. Costing just one or two old pennies, they lasted till he'd long pedalled out of sight.

It seemed many years before certain profound mysteries unravelled to my blissful youth. For instance, why did Grandma put a blue bag into the wash tub to make her whites whiter? Why wasn't Ibstock's High Street called Low Street when it was at the bottom of the village? and when Grandma came chasing me brandishing the clothes prop, why did she holler, "I'll murder you, my boy," when she knew people hang for less? When I was noisy she'd tell me to shut up, yet when I was quiet she'd cock her head suspiciously, saying, "You're up to mischief, aren't you?" Grown-ups were a real puzzle.

Grandad was an avid rabbit breeder and entered his prize rabbits in all the local shows. He frequently took me, from an early age, to his beloved exhibitions, which were invariably located in drinking houses. After astonishingly observing one man downing five pints of ale in quick succession, I remember feeling absurdly sympathetic. I said to Grandad, quite innocently, "Poor bloke - has his well run dry?"

Grandad was very proud of his rabbits. A few nights before a show, he would put them on the table and groom them till their fur sparkled. His equipment was an old silk garment discarded by Grandma - an old scarf, an underskirt, silk stockings rolled tightly. He'd say, "Blow out the candle." In the darkness the static electricity fairly crackled as he stroked and we'd watch in awe as sparks flashed off the fur. Grandad kept English and Dutch varieties. His ambition was to one day breed the perfect specimen. Our sheds were lined with hundreds of certificates and rosettes, a legacy to a lifetime of dedication. Grandma didn't share his enthusiasm. "Damn things," she'd moan, "attracting the flies to the house."

One day Grandad went through hell. He found many of the prize rabbits lying dead. He blamed a fox for the cunning way it had broken open the hutches. They were made of light chicken wire stretched over home-made wooden frames. The fox had taken its pick and left the other dead animals strewn everywhere. Grandad's eyes became bright with tears. A lifetime of dedication destroyed in one night.

Grandad's second love was his prize bantams. We were never short of miniature brown eggs for breakfast, with their rich, dark yolk. Occasionally, the hens would lay soft-shelled eggs - but Grandad had the answer. "Save all your eggshells," he'd say at breakfast time. "Crush them up finely and we'll mix them in with the corn feed." The hens would happily eat the shells, which promptly cured the problem. Nature's recycling system, I thought.

Being a farm worker meant Grandad had access to ample corn feed. He would keep the grain in a large hessian sack in his shed but at this particular time the sack always seemed to sprout a hole. No matter how many times he changed the sack, next morning he'd find a trickle of corn on the floor.

He borrowed a trap from the farm and set it. Next morning we hurried to see the result. Sure enough, the trap held something in its jaws - something we weren't expecting. "A rat's leg?" I asked in surprise. Grandad nodded. What he said next made me shudder with revulsion. "The rat has bitten off its own leg to escape," he said grimly. "I've known it before."

Many months later we witnessed a remarkable sequel to this story. Already well past midnight, we heard this terrific commotion. Something was terrifying our bantams in the bottom outbuilding. Hurriedly, we left our beds to investigate. In our torch light we saw a large rat rampaging back and forth among prostrate bodies. The floor was littered with fatally maimed birds and now the vermin sought its escape but Grandad got it - stabbed it with the long cane of my fishing net but it wasn't until the cold morning light, when we were counting dead birds, that we noticed something decidedly odd - the rat we'd killed had one back leg missing. The puzzle that had haunted us for months suddenly became crystal clear - this was the very rat we had previously caught in the corn shed.

A traditional cast iron open fireplace was the focal point of our living room. Every morning, before the fire was lit, Grandma's black leading ritual began. It was a hard, messy job, brushing the boiler and the oven until they sparkled like black mirrors but it was Grandma's pride and joy. So was the daily scrubbing of the red quarry-tiled kitchen floor.

We kept the fireside boiler topped up with rainwater carried from the butts outside. It always harboured daddy-long-legs and a variety of hideous larvae that fouled your face flannel but today's tap water couldn't touch it for soft, silky-smoothness. Preparation for a bath was a major operation. The fireside boiler held only about two gallons, so to supplement the meagre hot water supply, a cauldron was suspended from a hook over the fire. Our zinc bath was brought in and placed on the cold kitchen floor. We had no radiators to warm us. That kitchen must have been the coldest place this side of Siberia. All us children had to use the same water. A pecking order was established according to the grime factor. This invariably meant girls first, Frank last!

Oven temperature could be regulated only by heat from the fire. This often caused problems. For instance, Sunday's dinner wasn't complete without our Yorkshire pudding - we called it batter pudding. This needed a very hot oven to make it rise nicely, so in the height of summer we'd swelter in front of this roaring fire - all for the sake of our Sunday pud.

My Childhood in Ibstock by Iris Gleeson

I was born at 14 Melbourne Road, Ibstock on 10th May 1932, the third daughter of Fred and Gertrude Storer, in the front room of the house where my grandmother, Sarah Storer, lived with the rest of her family.

Our little family occupied the front room which as you can imagine was not very roomy. In fact I was told later that this room had originally been a fish and chip shop and the pans had been removed when Mum and Dad came to live there when my eldest sister was a small child.

At this time council houses were being built in Leicester Road, Ibstock and I have always maintained that I was the means of the family receiving the key to 168, Leicester Road, as the midwife thought that we were very cramped.

We had a good childhood, not much money but lots of love. We three children attended the Wesleyan Chapel which was at the top of the hill from where Grandma lived, and we would leave home to attend the morning service, going to Grandma's for lunch, returning for Sunday School in the afternoon, before going home to tea with Mum and Dad. This carried on until I was about five years of age.

During this time it was decided to buy a new organ for the chapel. An extension was needed to house this. The bricks to carry out the work were sold for 6d each, with your name printed on it, so if you go and look at the side of the chapel opposite The Oak public house, you can see my name along with that of my sisters, aunts, uncles, cousins etc.

When I was about five years old my older sisters decided that they did not want to carry on going to Grandma's, so it was decided that we should transfer to the Baptist Chapel in Chapel Street as we could return home between services. This suited us well and the association with the Baptist Chapel carried on and we always 'sat up' at the Anniversary services. It took me many years to get to the top row as I was small and we sat according to size. It was at these services that I first sang a solo, singing later at evening services. I transferred to the choir at sixteen and continued for many years, even after I left the village. I even returned to the chapel for my wedding in March 1967.

On Summer evenings, while we were still small, Mother used to take us for a walk. These took several different directions. We walked into Ravenstone to collect bluebells at the side of the road near to Hardy's farm, where we used to call to ask for a drink of water, whether we needed one or not, as the water was direct from a well and very cold. Another walk was along Richmond Road, down Blackberry Lane which was an un-made road, and out onto the Ravenstone Road and back across the fields belonging to the Baker family. This cut off the corner near to the Lastacrete.

We could, of course, take a walk by the Lastacrete, as on the other side there was a path which led to the side of the old mine workings, and occasionally we would find the bricked up tops of the shafts and drop down a pebble to see how long it took to reach the water. This area was known to us as the 'Ballysole', and it was not until many years later that I realised that it meant the ballast hole, as ashes etc. had been tipped there over the years. We did, on our adventures, find things which had been thrown away and, at one time, my sister Edna found a small white item which was, I later found out, a fairing. It showed a little boy sitting on a toilet but I just forget the saying printed on it. Oh to still have it now! Fond memories.

There were many other walks. Round the Bar, as it was known, along the fields from Overton Road, or via Harrison's Yard, over the brook which, as I remember, we called The Four Leaves, I do not know why, and along the brook. You could either come out at the bottom of Grange Road, or travel further along and come out opposite The Gas House. This was where the gas was made for the village, by burning coal, and you could see the gasometer at different levels depending on how much gas was being made or used.

When I reached my early teens, I still attended the Baptist Chapel and belonged to a group of young people who moved round the chapels, as we belonged to different ones. After the service had finished, we used to go for a walk, anything up to 20 to 25 of us, all about the same age. These walks were down into Heather by one road and back along another one, or into Ravenstone and back, and if we were feeling extra energetic, we would walk 'up the bar', along the road past the Nailstone Colliery, and perhaps call at the Neville Arms for a drink of pop before returning to Ibstock via Ellistown, if it were dark, or along the bridle path which runs from the top of Ellistown to Pretoria Road where we would go our separate ways to our homes in Leicester Road, Melbourne Road, Pretoria Road etc. This same group sometimes went to Coalville Pictures. The one film I remember was The Bells of St Mary when one of the girls wept right through it as she thought it was so sad. Not many dry eyes among the girls as you can guess. Sometimes if we stayed to see the end of the film, it would mean that we had to walk home to Ibstock as the last bus left Coalville at about 10pm.

I started school at the infants in Grange Road and can remember my first day, as my friend who lived next to me and was a week younger, cried all day, but I really enjoyed it. My first teachers were Mrs Shilcock and Miss Harratt. Miss Harratt also taught me during the second year and I can vividly remember her teaching us our manners which I have never forgotten. The other teachers at the infants were Miss Holmes, Miss Wyatt or White, who later became Mrs Harratt. The Head Teacher was Miss Lander. The school, at that time, was heated with pot-bellied stoves and when I smell plasticine now, it reminds me of my time at the school, as the balls used to be put at the side of the stove so that you could use them. We used to play the usual games and these included running after the boys and kissing them. I suppose this still goes on.

I moved to the junior school in 1939 just before the outbreak of the Second World War. The teacher in my first year was another Miss Harratt, I believe an aunt of my first teacher, and the headmaster was Mr Harratt. Second year was Miss Abell, third year Mrs Woolerton and last year Miss Johnson. This was a very good school where we had a grounding in the three Rs, together with singing, dancing etc. In fact, when I was about ten I was sent to the cloakroom one afternoon to teach Frank Gregory the steps, but he had two left feet, and as far as I know, still has. Sorry Frank!

I took the eleven plus examination and moved to King Edward VII Grammar School in September 1943, soon after my sister Linda was born. I stayed there for five years until 1948, not a very good pupil, just about average. During that time, my love of music continued, and I belonged to the choir for several years. Each year we had a music and drama festival and I sang duets and solos and took part in most of the plays ranging from comedy to heavy drama which was most enjoyable. I still

69

continue singing to this day in a choir, both in Coalville, and with my church.

I had two other sisters, one born when I was six years old, and our family returned to 14 Melbourne Road for the event. This was my sister, Constance Mary, known as Mary, who at the age of eighteen was married and moved to Canada, where she still lives. My youngest sister, Barbara, was born in May 1947 at Leicester Road, and one of my fondest memories of her was when she was May Queen at Bardon School which has now been pulled down to make an extension to the quarry. We had by this time moved from Ibstock to Bardon Road Club in Coalville where my mother and dad were steward and stewardess.

My only brother was born in April 1960 at Leicester Road and on the occasion my mother was attended by Dr Watts and Nurse Benton. Mother had six daughters and both her and Father had longed for a son. Dr Watts had said that if this was not a son he had thoughts of putting it back where it came from. Ha Ha! I do not know who was the most excited, but the doctor shouted down to us all waiting downstairs, "It's a boy!" It took some time to sink in.

I have many more happy memories of time and life in Ibstock, of boyfriends dancing at the Scout Hall, Working Men's Club etc., visits to Leicester for the yearly panto at The Opera House with the bus from Windridge Son & Riley, of the other bus companies, such as Hipwells, which then became Brown's Blue, Rudin Bros, and later the Victory Coaches.

Anon

I have lived in Ibstock all my life. Born in the forties I have seen many changes. I can remember going to school when the war was on. I can also remember rationing and clothing coupons. There used to be a grocery shop along the High Street called Cyril Greasley's and we used to have to go and queue for bananas and all kinds of things, when my mum heard that they had come in. Money was a bit tight in those days, so we didn't really have any luxuries. We had sweet coupons and I can remember this lady coming to our house and she used to swap with my mum sweet coupons for margarine and fats. We called that lady Mrs Can-I-Come-In?, as that was what she used to shout when she came to the door.

We lived in a terraced house, there were only two rooms up and two down. We hadn't got a proper kitchen, we had only got this stone sink and no running water. We had to draw the water from a pump on the backyard. I remember when they delivered the coal, my mum used to get it in and she used to have to take it through the front door and we used to store it under the stairs, in the cubby hole. Also, when the war was on we used to go under there when the sirens used to go off and wait there until the 'all clear'.

As there were only a few televisions around you used to have to make your own fun. We used to play on the road as there weren't many cars, we used to skip and play with an old bike wheel. We used to roll it and hit it with a stick. The one thing that sticks out in my mind is having a whip and top and Dad burning a pattern on it with a hot poker, then we used to colour it with chalk.

Across from where I lived was a farm so we used to go across there and help out when we could. The daughter of the farmer ran it and I sometimes used to go with her on the horse and cart delivering milk and sometimes when they were hay carrying we used to get to go on the tractor and dray. That used to be great fun. When they were hay carrying we used to go across and watch the threshing machine and then we would, sometimes, help to stack the hay if it wasn't too high.

We went to the Palace once a week, that's all my parents could afford. There used to be two houses on a Saturday night and we used to go to what they called the 'threepenny rush'. Mum used to give us some money and we used to go to Collier's Sweet Shop and get a few sweets. Some of the kids used to take either monkey nuts or cob nuts and used to crack them when it was all quiet, that used to send the owner mad. He used to come along the rows with his torch and threaten to throw you out if he could find the culprit.

Like a good many more families we didn't have much money but we had fun. In those days people stuck together more and they used to help one another.

Anon

I can remember the Ibstock Wakes, which used to be held on the field behind the Palace Cinema and the Ram Inn before they built the houses and bungalows known as the Fairfield Estate. I can remember as a child watching the big lorries loaded with all sorts of rides and stalls coming along High Street. I can remember, when I was engaged to my late husband, winning a china tea service and a canteen of cutlery on one of the stalls. The Wakes week was a big occasion in the village. It was always held round about the week-end of October 11th and people used to come from surrounding villages.

Another childhood memory is the Saturday afternoon matinee at the Palace Cinema. My mother used to give us a sixpence and we used to spend some of it on sweets to take into the cinema or save some of it and buy some chips from Mrs Moreton's fish and chip shop, after we came out.

Inside the Palace, it was just bedlam when the film started whether it was a cowboy film or some other adventure story, and there would be foot stamping and shouting

film or some other adventure story, and there would be foot stamping and shoutin
when the Indians or the villain came on the screen. Mr Ball, the owner of th
cinema, would come round with his torch and threaten to throw you out if yo
didn't behave and keep quiet.

The Palace Cinema

The Sunday School Anniversary was always looked forward to when I was a chil
in the forties. We used to go to the Primitive Chapel in Curzon Street, my tw
brothers, my sister and myself. We used to go three times on that day. That was th
only time we ever had any new clothes, as my mum had a struggle trying to cloth
four children at that time. She could never afford to have anything new herself bu
she always made sure we looked smart. We used to go into the neighbours nex
door to show off our outfits. I can remember I loved to have black patent shoes an
white socks.

Also, when I was a girl I used to have an evening paper round. I used to start i
Curzon Street, go along Meadow Row, this was a long row of houses wher
Springfield Close is today, down Spring Road and right to the top of Pretoria Road

ll for the princely sum of 1/6d a week - twelve and a half pence in today's money and on Friday I used to have to collect the money. My youngest brother used to help me to deliver them sometimes, then I used to have to give him half of my wages.

In the Winter we would take a sledge, made for us by my dad. We used to have very bad winters then and lots of snow, sometimes it would cover the hedges. My youngest sister would come with us and we would pull the sledge up to the top of Pretoria Road, locally called Common Hill, and then we would come down on the sledge. We didn't worry about the traffic as not many cars could get on the road because of the snow.

Remember by Pamela Allen

My earliest memory of growing up, in what was then a very tightly-knit community, the smell of freshly baked bread coming from Mee's Bakery near to where I lived in the High Street.

Going down 'The Street', as it was and still is called, I remember sounds and smells. Saturday morning (after the 3d rush to see the Cisco Kid at the Palace) walking down the Street, Lawrence's drapery shop - the smell of fresh linen and polish, the hairdresser's - the sudden waft of perming solution (what were those great iron clips used for??). The smell of fresh cut wood from Harratt's wood yard and the sound of the circular saw. My grandad kept his hand cart in Mr Harratt's big shed. He used it to deliver furniture around the village.

I remember the grocer's and the rows of biscuits in tins, the smell of cheese and bacon. When we went to The Star I always made a beeline for the chairs that were there for the customers to rest on and have a chat. The paper shop across the road, the shoe shop and the smell of fresh leather from the cobbler's. The butchers, the pubs, the millinery shop, the 'tin' shop, the watch mender's. The Post Office, all along the High Street right down to Crane's Farm and Manton's Corner.

I remember Mrs Moreton's fish and chip shop. The smell of salt and vinegar, standing in the queue on a Saturday lunchtime, and buckets of chipped potatoes appearing from the back of the shop. I remember wondering "how do they make potatoes into chips?" whilst I was standing tracing patterns in the sawdust on the floor and the smell of steaming newspapers when someone asked for their order to be wrapped.

Spring - May was Sunday School anniversary time, the start of the cricket season. At our house Dad oiling his bat and whitening his cricket boots, being told not to touch! I remember the smell of linseed oil and whitening, and leather batting gloves. Cricket boots standing out to dry against the back door on a Sunday.

Sunday School, given hymn sheets, and told to keep them clean, going home wi all the intention of doing so, and covering them with left-over wall paper.

The big day, the Sunday School Anniversary, the Chapel is full and the big doo separating the main chapel and the Sunday School room are opening up to let : the congregation in, platforms reaching to the ceiling. Then a hush, Mr Underwoo stands up and all the choir rise to their feet (I remember thinking, I hope the platforms hold), and the lovely singing and music, heaven knows how it all seeme to come together right on the day.

Summer - School holidays, did the sun always shine then? Sunday School outings Wicksteed Park, playing down the brook, taking jam sandwiches and a bottle water down Locker's Lane (Overton Road) to go fishing and paddle in the for Looking for watercress in the brook that ran through the fields near the ford. Bein run off for swinging in the hedges in the Ram field; playing cricket, making dens the field. The children who lived along the High Street, Orchard Street and th 'Black Pad' used the field as a recreation ground.

Autumn - The Wakes (the Fair) held on the Ram field. It was always Holland's Fu Fair. I remember the smell of diesel fumes from the generators that ran the ligh and the rides. The sweet smell of ginger bread and candy floss. The sky used to b lit up from the fair and the sound of the music could be heard quite a distanc away. November - Bonfire Night, and the biggest bonfire ever, always seemed to b on The Ram field. Weeks of collecting rubbish to burn from everyone in the villag Always lots of fireworks and always a guy that was paraded along the High Stre while collecting pennies for the guy.

Winter - December, the build up to Christmas. School parties, bring your own kni and fork, and spoon. Sunday School parties, with coloured cotton wound rour cutlery so that you knew which was yours when it came to home time. The shop down the Street full of Christmas goodies - Mr Hall always had a splendid collectio of dolls, with a big crinoline doll in the middle. Restall's, the chemist's windov filled with lavender bath cubes, Evening in Paris and California Poppy perfume i lovely boxes. Every shop all the way down the Street decorated for Christmas. remember.......

Starting School by Paula Gretton

In September 1960 when I started school, the Infant School was not where it is nowadays at the back of the Junior School. It was situated in Grange Road. It is still standing there but now it is a private residence. The school comprised of three classrooms and in the Top classroom there was a little office partition for Mrs Hutchinson, the headmistress and Mrs Shilcock, the school secretary.

I can remember so clearly the day I started school. My next door neighbour and I both went happily and excitedly as we skipped along Central Avenue and down the jitty on that warm September morning. Our mums took us, that very first morning anyway, and went in the classroom with us. Our teacher was called Mrs De Vere. She looked lovely and she was. The right sort of person for an infant teacher, pretty, kind and gentle, but very firm. Woe betide anyone who misbehaved. They would surely find themselves standing in the corner with their face to the wall.

We were given little pink or blue cardboard badges for our mums to write our names on. I couldn't understand why some of the children were crying. As I looked round I saw all sorts of different things. There was the sand tray and the water tray, a Wendy House in the corner, a bookcase full of Janet and John books with cushions in front of it , a painting corner. I was wishing all the mums would go home so that we could explore the delights of school.

At last the mums had gone, only one or two of the children were still crying, and Mrs De Vere called the register to see if everyone had turned up. We were given some paper and fat crayons on which to draw a picture of a sunny day. At break time we went out to play in the playground, after having had a little bottle of milk and some biscuits (they tell me the milk at school now comes in little cartons! Not the same, is it?).

After break, Mrs De Vere showed us all the things in the classroom and told us how, in the next few months, we would learn to read and write and do sums. What fascinated me was the Nature Table. She wanted the children to bring something to put on the table, and at this time of the year the table would be full of blackberries, conkers, acorns and leaves of many different varieties and colours.

At 12 o'clock, some of the children started to line up at the gate, but not me or my friend. Our mums had come to take us home for dinner. We found out later that the children lining up were the 'dinner babies', and they were walked up High Street and Chapel Street to the Scout Hut on Leicester Road, where they would have their dinner.

Such was the freedom, even that short while ago, our mums let us go back to school on our own. We ran down Central Avenue and skipped down the jitty, taking care not to tread on any cracks, to the bottom where the lollipop man was waiting.

In the afternoon, we listened to a story on the radio then we all folded our arms on

our desks, laid down our heads, closed our eyes and went to sleep for ten minute
Why we did this I don't know. I do know, however, I was impatient to discov
more of the wonders of the classroom. We played with some thick wooden bead
threading them on laces, sorting out the colours and counting them. I knew fro
the very first day I was going to like school.

As the days passed, the weeks went into months, and it felt to me that this wa
where I belonged. Of course, everything was not always sweetness and light. The
was always a black cloud for me at the Infant School, because I could not sing
tune. Mrs Hutchinson used to ask you to sing for her and then she said if you we
a 'singer' or a 'growler'. I cried when she told me I was to stand with the growler
When we had assembly or hymn practice she would sometimes stop the singin
and say, "Now we want to hear it sung properly, so growlers don't sing." I wa
really ashamed to think I was spoiling the singing, and I still can't sing!

Safely in the 60s by Dawn Bryans

Earliest memories for me start around being at the Infants School that used to b
down Grange Road in the village. I only lived about ten minutes away at a chilc
pace so I can remember my mum took me on the first day and after that I walked
school with whoever I happened to be friends with that week. We were never to
not to speak to strangers or not to get into cars or go off with anyone we didr
know because there wasn't any need. The only evil or wicked people I was awa
of existed only in stories or in my own imagination. The only danger that wa
immediate was in crossing the road at the bottom of the street.

I can remember we used to have to drink milk in half pint bottles with a straw ar
in the winter the milk used to freeze in the bottles and it forced the foil top off so
looked like a milk lollipop. The milk was thawed out next to the boilers in th
classroom so it was never cold to drink.

In the playground we used to play all sorts of games that involved much runnin
about or jumping up and down. There was a 'kiss chase' that involved someor
being 'it' and running after whoever they wanted to kiss and trying to catch them
kiss them whether they wanted to be kissed or not and that person took over th
chasing. We used to form a crocodile of children in pairs and skip around th
playground singing, "The Big Ship Sails Round the Alley Alley O" and to this da
I've never found out where the Alley Alley O was to be found. Someone wou
often bring a long skipping rope and we could take it in turns to turn either end
allow others to run in and out or skip fast or slow but if they were the cause of th
rope stopping turning, they had to take a turn at either end.

The school holidays always meant long hot sunny days spent doing a variety lings from going on picnics to the brook that runs across the road down Locker's Lane (Overton Road) to walking without parents, to Coalville Baths, for a swim in the pool that was on Avenue Road.

For picnics my friends and I would pack up butter and sugar sandwiches and a bottle of water along with our bathing costumes and a towel and would often be gone for quite some time with no-one worrying too much about how long we were gone. The only rule I can think of was that I never went anywhere alone in case I hurt myself. More often than not my younger brother tagged along as well. We also used to go on long walks across fields and down long winding lanes and play games along the way imagining we were kings and queens and fairies and witches, making the stories up as we went along. The fields were full of daisies and buttercups so we would see who could make the longest chain from these flowers and then we would wear them in our hair or around our necks for as long as they lasted. These were the days before we owned a bike so therefore we walked everywhere. I still walk 'round the Bar' (Belchers' Bar) now with my dogs and very often smile to myself when I go past the hedges and trees we used to run in and out of, living some adventure or charmed life we used to imagine.

When we got back to the village we would walk through the Churchyard looking at the gravestones to find the oldest one there. Pagets' tomb always frightened us because of stories we were told by older children so when we came near it our feet would develop wings and we would run like the wind to get as far away as possible from it.

There were always fields to play in and we were especially lucky to have a brook in one of them. This was on Spring Lane before the industrial units were there. The trees and hedges grew either side of the brook so if we weren't fishing for minnows and tadpoles, someone would climb one of the trees and tie a rope or a discarded cable to one of the branches. We would then take it in turns to swing across the brook by way of this rope. Many times have I fallen in because I let go of the rope or the rope itself snapped, depositing me in the middle of the brook and hoped that I could get dry before I went home so I wouldn't be told off or made to stay in by way of punishment. Quite often we would see how many of us could swing on the rope at the same time so you could guarantee the rope was going to break and we would get a soaking.

My brother and I had a friend who lived about five doors up from us and his dad kept chickens in their back garden. Our houses used to back onto Beesons' orchard before it was later developed into a housing estate. We would let the chickens out into the orchard and spend hours trying to catch them to put them back into their run. This would involve chasing the chickens and climbing trees trying to retrieve them to put them back safely. We knew how many there were and there was many a last minute scramble to get the last one back before it started to get late and time for them to be fed by our friend's dad.

After tea time other adventures would take all sorts of forms, without our paren
having to pay any money out. If we wanted any money at all we could be sure o
finding empty pop bottles to take back to the Off Licence that used to be at th
bottom of the jitty on High Street. Or if someone hadn't been there first, you coul
guarantee to find money behind the Ram pub where drunks would fall over an
lose money from their pockets. After finding some money we would go to the ch
shop and share two shillings worth. If we were feeling a bit naughty there was
game called 'Tommy knocking' that would amuse and frighten us at the same tim
This involved walking past a row of houses and knocking on the door of perha
two or three and running off before anyone opened the door. I remember runnir
off plenty of times with my heart in my mouth at the thought of someone catchir
up with us to give us a clip round the ear, and hoping that they didn't recognise u
so our parents wouldn't get to know.

Getting towards the end of the school holidays we would go looking f
blackberries, armed with jars and bowls of different descriptions. I don't think ar
of us came back very often with many because we would eat more than we actual
brought home.

Mondays would always be wash day for mums so my friends and I would alwa
try to be out of the way when this occurred because the old methods of washir
tended to take up the whole day. All clothes were washed, beds were stripped an
all whites were boiled in a copper that tended to boil over causing lots of stea
and bubbles. I remember my mum had what she called a copper stick with whic
my brother and I were threatened many times but luckily for us we never receive
The fear of being on the receiving end of that was deterrent enough for us. As I'v
mentioned earlier, the weather always seemed to be fine and warm so the washir
was always dried and more often than not sheets were put back on beds the sam
day they were taken off, bearing in mind there were at least three beds in ou
house.

On Wednesdays when the Co-op Baker used to deliver the bread, Mum would bu
us a jam or cream doughnut so my brother and I would make sure we were alway
at home on this particular day. We would wait until Dad came home from work s
we could all eat them together.

Friday nights my brother and I received our pocket money and thinking back w
got half-a-crown each. We would immediately go down the road to Hall's which
still there, but when we used to visit the shop it sold toys and games at variou
prices. I remember there was a lady who worked in there and she always had a l
of patience with us while we tried to make up our minds what to spend our mone
on.

Books could be borrowed from the library that was and still is at the High Schoo
Saturday mornings would always be spent at the library looking at and choosir
our individual reading material for the next fortnight at least. I can remembe

eading about Noddy, Torchy and books by Enid Blyton such as the Famous Five. Sometimes at night-time my parents would take us to the British Legion Club that used to be on High Street where we would meet up with friends to either play outside or join in the dancing to various groups or bands who came to entertain everyone. Bingo would be played for a short time so we were always made to be quiet whilst this was in progress.

Sunday mornings we would go to Chapel and again meet up with our friends to sing hymns and listen to stories from the Bible. At a certain time of year we would have what we called Sermons where we would practise singing songs to perform in front of our parents and relatives. We would be seated on a platform with the older children sitting at the top and smaller children nearer the bottom so that they wouldn't hurt themselves if they did happen to fall off. My sisters and I always had a new dress and shoes to wear for these Anniversaries so we didn't mind singing for everyone.

Sunday nights was always bath night in our house and at this time we didn't have a bathroom so water was boiled in the copper and then transferred to a tin bath which was placed in front of the fire. We would take it in turns to have a bath. There was always plenty of hot water despite having to heat it first. If the weather was warm in the daytime the bath would be taken outside in the garden and filled with cold water so we could play in it.

can't remember being bored or fed up during my childhood because there was always something to do or somewhere to go. If the weather was too cold to be outside I would go to a friend's house or she would come to mine where we played with dolls, again imagining some fairy tale and dressing them accordingly. We would often make clothes for the dolls ourselves from scraps of material and any unwanted wool that we could find around the house.

On thinking about how things were then and how they are now I suppose, as children, we were quite lucky in that we had lots to do to amuse ourselves. Our parents didn't have the money to buy everything we wanted and I can't remember thinking of anything that I really wanted but couldn't have. Television wasn't as entertaining as it is now for children so I can't say that we watched all that much. The only things I can remember seeing was Watch with Mother with characters like Bill and Ben, Tales of the Riverbank, The Woodentops and Andy Pandy. Games that we played outside included Hopscotch, Tick, Hide and Seek. We would make dens out of clothes airers and blankets and then pretend all sorts of things from being mums and dads to being schoolteachers. I don't think we were ever stuck for something to do because we were used to having to think for ourselves and not rely on computer games and the television to keep us entertained. It makes you wonder who is the luckiest, the children today who have to be amused, or those of us who could amuse ourselves at no expense. Today there are a lot of restrictions with regards to children's safety in that they can't just go off to wander through fields and woods like we used to do, or go anywhere that matters without being under their parents' supervision. I would like to think that younger children have got older brothers or sisters with some imagination and the time to spend with them, to enjoy the outdoors and countryside, although even that is being taken up these days for housing estates and industrial units. There is still some countryside left if you know where to look for it.

Ibstock Memories by Betty Stiles

My Ibstock memories are of working at Ibstock County Junior School in the 60s. The Headmistress, Ethel Simpson, ensured that standards of both learning and behaviour were excellent and special events were always carefully organised. Uniforms were encouraged, with black blazers bearing the school badge, a bird entwined with the 'I' of Ibstock. On school outings the children looked as smart as many a fee-paying school.

One Easter we took a party of ten-year-olds to Paris, quite an innovation in those days. There was great excitement with parents and friends seeing us off on the coach outside school. Unfortunately fog had held up the plane due to take us from Castle Donington that morning so we spent the day there with various messages being relayed back to Ibstock saying we would be going, no we wouldn't, etc! East Midlands Airport was in its very early days and had no restaurant or snack bar, just the one large waiting hall. The staff took the children on a tour of the hangars, much to their delight, then we were served with fish and chips in the Staff Canteen - very welcome but not the best meal for excited children, as we learned to our cost on eventually flying off that evening!

Sports Days were always very special occasions, organised to the last T and everything well rehearsed, including the parade of all competitors round the field. There were four houses, Swift, Swallow, Martin and Kingfisher. Each house had a different colour, blue, red, green, and yellow. The House Captain led the house team round the field carrying the appropriate house banner aloft. A good crowd of mothers and fathers always gave support to the entrants. One year Lady Fiennes, mother of Sir Ranulph, presented the prizes on Sports Day, quite a 'coup' for a small village school but Miss Simpson had met her many years before and they always kept in touch. The afternoon finished with tea in school for the invited guests, school governors, etc. As Miss Simpson always provided delicious cream pastries from 'Elisabeth the Chef', many of us had a suspicion that this was more of an attraction than watching the races.

Staff, in those days, were always very generous with their time out of school hours. The Deputy Head, Ron Hughes, would rehearse his choir and dancers at lunch time or after school. Hilda Bevin, later Hilda Bodicoat, would work tirelessly to produce ctors for the Nativity Play each year and, with Ron Hughes, would produce a Carol service of really high quality.

The school orchestra flourished, mainly violins, and many youngsters went on to the County Youth Orchestra, achieving pleasure and success. One tradition, still remembered by most ex-pupils from those days, was the Friday morning hymn practice when Mr Hughes kept the whole school in the hall after morning prayers to practise hymns. Although playing the piano, he had an eagle eye for miscreants and woe betide those who did not attend or misbehaved in any way.

These may be memories of thirty years ago but I think they will be vivid still to many Ibstock adults.

Gloria Barwell

I would like to write to you about my gran who won the Land Army Victory Cross, the only woman in Leicestershire to have won this award. My gran's name was Mrs Daisy Archer. Before she married she lived at number 10 Leicester Road, Ibstock. One of nine children of Agnes and Robert Lardner, the only girl.

The story begins in the village of Finedon in Northamptonshire. My gran was serving in the Land Army, the year was 1919, the month was June. There was a railway strike at the time, and the groom of a titled county person was delivering two horses to a race meeting. She was walking along the road at the time when the groom was thrown into the air. As she saw them coming she went into action. She stopped them after they had dragged her about half a mile.

On November 22, 1919 at Throgmorton Hall, London the Princess Royal presented her with the Land Army V.C. and her picture appeared in the national newspapers. A heroine was made on that day in 1919.

Her last remaining years were spent at Westgate Old People's Flats, Ibstock. She is buried in Ibstock Churchyard. Ibstock should be proud of a very brave lady, as I am.

Note: There are only about six Land Army Victoria Crosses in the country that have been won. When my gran won this award she was 18 years of age.

An Evacuee's Tale by Ray Dace

I came to live in Ibstock in November 1940 - although I nearly didn't make it
Dench's House Trust in Birmingham, next to my home, was the victim of
bombing raid, so we were all lined up at the school on Ravenhurst Road ready t
catch the bus to Ibstock to be evacuated. However, my friend Brian and I, althoug
only six and four years old, decided to escape. So we ran off and hid in the bombe
out houses until the bus had to leave without us. I remember us playing an
sleeping in the ruins, and we tried to salvage a red pedal car which was burie
under the debris, and of course no one came looking for us as they thought w
were on the bus. However, the next day, Miss Eames appeared and carted us off t
Ibstock in a very sorry state.

The first night we spent with Mr Dolman, but the following day we were separated
and I was taken to Mr and Mrs Dace in Chapel Street, where they and their son Jac
and daughter Barbara made a great fuss of me and before long I had a new mur
and dad and a brother and sister. After I had been bathed and dressed in decer
clothes I was taken to the National School in High Street, where all the evacuee
were taken to be assessed, and put in the care of Miss Harratt who was kind an
compassionate.

Unfortunately the terrors of the raids on Birmingham remained for some time
apparently I was prone to dive under the nearest table or desk at the sound of
siren, or the drone of an aeroplane overhead. I don't think I could have seen o
heard a radio until I came to live at Ibstock and I later learned that I was botl
alarmed and then fascinated by it.

We made our own amusement in those days, and would wander down the fields fo
a picnic, with a bottle of cold tea and sandwiches, spending many happy hour
along the brook which runs through to Overton Road, both jumping it an
paddling. Late Summer we would collect blackberries from the hedgerows for jan
and blackberry vinegar. Crab apples which grew wild were used for jelly.

My dad used to take me on the crossbar of his bike down to Shackerstone Canal t
teach me how to fish. I was introduced to the wonders of nature when he instille
in me a love of the birds, butterflies and plants we encountered en route. Like mos
miners he had a great fondness for the open air and relished each hour away forn
the depths of the mine. We always ended these trips by calling in at the Rising Sur
at Shackerstone for a bottle of lemonade, for me. He would have a glass of foaminj
beer which was brought up from the depths of the cellar in a stone jug - they didn'
have beer pumps then. During the Summer holidays we all had a stroll down t
Heather on a Sunday night after chapel, and used to call at the pub at the top of th
hill to sit in the garden with a bottle of Vimto and, if we were lucky, a bag of crisp

By this time Mr and Mrs Dace had learned that my mother had been lost after an ai
raid and, as my father was a lorry driver without means of caring for me, the

decided to adopt me. I was more than happy to learn of this, as I had no memory of any other home and family except Mum and Dad and my new brother and sister. Although my poor mum must often have wondered what she had let herself in for sometimes, as I did rather have a penchant for getting into trouble.

On one occasion I had disobeyed orders from the Senior School not to go down to the Annual Fair which was held on the Ram Inn field every October. Having slipped out of school and down the jitty into High Street, I ran onto the Ram Field and was immediately bitten by the owner's dog. Dr Meldrum said it served me right for being disobedient, and put four stitches into the back of my knee. I still have the scar to this day.

My next enterprise was collecting rosehips for the local chemist, Mr Restall, who used to give us 3d per jar. Those surplus to requirements came in very handy at school as itching powder, and resulted in much amusement and sore backs, (not to mention backsides which had been caned.) To get the powder out, the rosehips had to be split, and I was quietly sitting under the table, minding my own business, sorting mine out when I split my thumb open. Naturally, not daring to tell my mum, I kept quiet and the wound went septic. I expect I got a good hiding in the end anyway. The scar is still in evidence.

My piece de resistance was balancing on the back of a huge shire horse belonging to Archie Dawson who had a farm over the road from our house. My brother used to help out there, and I loved to go with him, delivering milk in cans at 1d a pint, and as a reward, being lifted onto the horse's back for a ride - but the horse was so broad and I was so short, it was a wonder I didn't fall off and break my neck.

Just up the road from us was the Baptist Chapel, where we all went three times every Sunday and, eventually, I used to pump the organ there for Mr Ellis Newbold. The chapel also provided us with many enjoyable social events, from whist drives and beetle drives to concerts, many of which were organised by my sister Barbara, who had a wonderful voice. I loved to be allowed to take an active part in these concerts and I remember two outstanding singers, Betty Morris and Vera Bott.

Of course we all looked forward to outings to Abbey Park in Leicester and, later on, Wicksteed Park and Drayton Manor. Probably the anticipation was the best part, all getting on the bus in a state of high excitement, clutching macs and picnics, and the sing-songs on the bus coming home.

Soon, however, tragedy struck. My father was killed after being crushed in an accident at Nailstone Colliery in 1945. Matters relating to my adoption were still afoot so, despite her own terrible loss, my mother still went ahead with the adoption, and on 20 June 1946 I changed my name from Raymond Wilfred Ward to Raymond Michael Dace. The Judge at Ashby Court very kindly asked if I was happy with my new name and when I told him I didn't like Wilfred, he gave permission for it to be changed to Michael. To help overcome the trauma of all this, my mother took me to Blackpool for a whole week's holiday and I recall entering a Talent

Contest playing the piano, and winning the second prize, a huge box of plasticine. I had been lucky enough to have been allowed piano lessons with both Miss Fox of High Street and Mr Brown of Copson Street, once I had settled into school at Ibstock. I have them to thank for doing well in the competition. The fact that my sister taught piano must also have helped me.

By this time I had made many friends in Ibstock, although some parents were still wary of evacuees and were not too keen for their children to associate with us. One notable exception were Mr and Mrs Ridgway, who made me welcome at their home any time, and I thought of them as a second family. Their son Ivan and I spent many happy hours around the lanes and fields, either walking or on our bikes. We used to cycle all the way to Tamworth to go swimming, and often used to walk to Coalville to the Baths. We spent many hours playing football on the Welfare on Leicester Road, but if we spotted the steam erupting from the Gas Works nearby we all had to stop whatever we were doing and dash home to collect wheelbarrows to go down to the gasworks for 6d worth of coke.

Another good source of fuel at that time were barrows of logs from Mr Harratt in High Street - I remember delivering some for him to the big house which later became the British Legion and being given a whole shilling tip from the owner. A lot of money then.

Tips and pennies from errands were hoarded to ensure getting in to the 3d rush at the Palace Cinema. Every week there was a serial, so we were always on good behaviour so that we would be allowed to attend, as failure to do so meant missing a vital part of the serial which was always on before the big film. Mr Ball owned the cinema. He would stroll menacingly up and down the aisles, to ensure there was not too much in the way of booing and catcalling at the villains on screen - or too much scuffling from those off screen come to that.

Sweet coupons permitting, we would call in at Mr Moreton's sweet shop which used to stand on the pavement outside the cinema, and treat ourselves to a bar of chocolate or a few sweets. Mind you, no-one sold toffee to compare with that made by my mother. She always made us a load for bonfire night, sugar rations permitting, and it could hold your jaw steady for hours. Mind you, the flavour was not to be forgotten.

Ivan and I then used to go next door to his Auntie Ivy, at Moreton's Fish and Chip Shop, and peel a few buckets of potatoes in return for a lovely fish supper. People queued from all over the place as their fish and chips were legendary. Of course, there were often potato or fat shortages at that time, but there were a number of fish and chip shops in Ibstock then: Moreton's, Chaplin's and Poxon's on High Street, King's on Melbourne Road, and another one in Chapel Street. There would always be some open.

There used to be numerous parades and fetes or Sunday School Parades in those days, usually led by Ernie Mee with the Red Garries. People rattled tins, collecting for the Hospital Fund. It's funny thinking back, but I'm sure the sun always shone and we never got rained off.

I did my own share of marching with the Boy Scouts led by Les Pike and both Ivan and I swam in the team at galas at Coalville. Ibstock Silver Prize Band was very popular then, and I used to play the euphonium, but after one very hot day in a parade at Markfield, I decided that my legs were too small and my euphonium too big, and switched over to playing the cornet.

Money was not easily come by then and, having spotted a gleaming Raleigh bicycle in Mrs Fowke's shop window in Chapel Street, I took on a couple of paper rounds to raise the money to buy it. I delivered for Arthur Burchell on Sundays and did a daily round for him. I also took the Leicester Mercury round in the evening for Windridge's.

Winter mornings and evenings must have been colder then - we had none of the protective lightweight clothes around today. Woolly balaclavas held out the cold and rain, and legs acquired a permanent red ring from the top of wet wellies up to legs of short trousers from about October to March. Long trousers were an unheard of luxury then - I longed for the day when I had my brother's to grow into.

Eventually, all good things come to an end, and I left Ibstock Secondary Modern School when I was fifteen with mixed feelings. They had not all been good times, obviously. I had had my share of bad days, probably more than some, but I enjoyed school on the whole. Despite the memory of my Dad, I started work at Nailstone Colliery as a blacksmith's striker to George Perry.

Not too many years later I met an Ibstock girl who was to become my wife at Ibstock Church in 1957.

Evacuees in Ibstock by Iris Gleeson

I was seven years old at the time of the outbreak of World War 2 and had just moved schools from Ibstock Infants to Ibstock Junior. War really was just another word to us at that age, as we did not see, or should I say, at that time realise what it was all about as our lives carried on as normal. I think that it was at the beginning of 1940 that evacuees arrived in our village and our family did not have any at that time, but some youngsters from the Birmingham area were billeted with some local families.

I lived in The Avenue on Leicester Road, which was a cul-de-sac of 14 houses, and at this time Jean Hunter came to live with Mr and Mrs Sharpe and their daughter Dorothy, my age, on the main road just round the corner from us. I believe there was also another girl named Doreen who only stayed a very short time. Mrs

Sharpe's son, George, was serving in the Army and her elder daughter was married to Mr Brown, one of the local butchers. Jean became a firm friend of my sister Doris, and even to this day she can still tell you her address in Birmingham. I think Jean stayed over twelve months.

Mr and Mrs Stirland, at the bottom of the Avenue, had staying with them two brothers, Peter and Barry Jackson, also from Birmingham and I particularly remember Barry as he was my first boyfriend. I was seven and he was six! They were a nice couple of lads as I remember them, but I think that Peter became a little rebellious and as the circumstances at home changed they returned there.

At school, I remember the name of Dennis Caffin or Kaffin, and he lived, I believe with Mr and Mrs Reed and their two children on Ashby Road, opposite Strawberry Villa, and it was at Strawberry Villa that we used to call for a pennyworth of apples from Mr and Mrs Gamble who had a big orchard and sold their 'fallers' to the children. Beautiful tasting ones as I recall, oh my taste buds!

In my class was a young lady by the name of Betty Williamson and she lived with Lawyer Newman and his wife and their daughter, Molly. I believe Betty stayed a number of years, as she was here when we took the eleven plus examination and moved to either Market Bosworth or Ashby Grammar School.

As you may appreciate, at that time we all had very distinct accents, from the very broad Ibstock to the Brummie twang, but Betty had a very refined voice and I am sure she came from the London area. One thing I recall is that when she was writing at her desk, her head would be almost touching the top and it seemed a very peculiar way, as most of us sat in the normal upright position. Funny little things stick in you memory!

Hilary and Lauriston Newman came to live with their grandmother in Station Road. They were not true evacuees but their father, who was an author, brother of Lawyer Newman above, worked in London. It could have been for one of the War Ministries and it was felt that they would be safer in Ibstock. Hilary was my age and I always envied her because she had beautiful long hair, naturally curly, and she either had it loose with a big bow or in plaits. I always wanted my hair plaited, but because it was so fine and wispy, mother would let it grow for a while, but when it became untidy, it was a case of snip, snip, straight round the bottom and a fringe. I did however, have my hair put in rags on Saturday night after the weekly bath, so I had ringlets on Sunday.

This now brings me to my little friend, Raymond Ward, who lived with Mr and Mrs Dace in Chapel Street, with Barbara Morris and Jack Hopton, and they all belonged to the Baptist Chapel which my family also attended. Barbara was, and still is, very musical and she used to organise the children and we would have concerts, in the school room upstairs at the chapel, to raise money for charities such as Red Cross Soldiers' Comfort Fund etc. These were very enjoyable times, both for the ones taking part and the people watching. The concerts were very varied and we used to

86

perform plays both comic and more serious, tap dancing, acrobatics, action songs, recitations, ballet etc. Raymond was a natural comic and we did one play called 'The Wrong Side of the Bed', in which he had to be in the bed, and one night he fell out of it and right off the stage. I seem to remember that he just got up, walked up the steps at the back of the stage, and climbed back into bed. As you can imagine, it caused a great laugh. He also had the habit of putting his hand over his face and moving it up and down and changing his expression as he did so. Raymond stayed on and was eventually adopted by Mrs Dace and he married an Ibstock girl and I think they now live in Nailstone. As he grew older he used to attend the same dances as myself and on occasions, escorted me safely home from the Scout Hall.

This leads me on to another family who came to live in The Avenue about 1941/42. This was a double family, the Burchells. There was Grandma and her daughters Edie and Clare, and their daughters Clara, Peggy, Betty and Anne and Diane. Their fathers, Frank and Don, were also brothers and their father was husband to Grandma. The two mothers worked at Ibstock Brick and Tile in the pipe works. The eldest girl, Clara, was my best friend, and still is, and we all took part in the Chapel Concerts and Anniversary Services. All the family stayed in Ibstock and still live there. A little later in the war, Anne joined the Ace Concert Party of which my father and myself were members, and sang such numbers as 'My Curly Headed Baby'. We were all able to tap dance and for a short while attended Madame Thirlby's dancing classes in the rooms at the top of Grange Road. The Burchell family had first lived in Orton-on-the-Hill near Twycross before moving to Ibstock.

Jimmy and Brian Clowes lived with Mr and Mrs Hall, the local electrician, although after a while Jimmy returned home but Brian stayed on and was eventually adopted by Mr and Mrs Hall and he still carries on their business, opposite The Palace Picture House.

My mother and father had three lots of evacuees, two at the same time. The first ones, Florrie and John Weston, were from London and they had been living with my Auntie Rose and Uncle Joe King at Nailstone, but due to the fact that my aunt's friend was coming out of hospital to stay with her and she had TB, it was felt that it would not be healthy for a young baby to be there. Florrie had a sister Lilian and her mother who came to visit us several times. My mother used to look after John while his mother went out to work. John cried a lot when he was hungry but as soon as a spoon went near his mouth, quietness reigned. Florrie and John stayed with us for a couple of years.

At the same time we had two brothers living with us from Birmingham, but originally they had lived with their mum and dad in my Aunt Lyd's house, next to Grandma Storer, in Melbourne Road. When the parents decided to return to Birmingham, Billy and Timmy Bache came to stay with our Aunt Emily, who kept a small shop at the top of Church Hill, nearly opposite Grandma's.

87

I cannot remember all the day to day happenings at that time, but recall that our family had always eaten their pudding before the main meal, which was the local custom in those days, and our visitors had been used to having the main meal first. In the end it was decided by mother that we all had to eat the main meal followed by pudding, and of course we still all do that now.

As you will appreciate, rationing was with us at that time and everyone had to make the most of whatever they had, and my mother used to make rhubarb and date jam, which I could not eat because of the colour of it, which was very brown, but the boys used to really enjoy it. Mother also used to 'make do and mend' which meant that if a garment was passed onto her which did not fit any of us, she would unpick it, wash it, and on her trusty old Singer sewing machine, would turn it into another garment to fit one of us.

At the weekends while the boys were with us, their older sisters and one of their friends used to visit, and as they came from a large town and we were only country folks, their clothes would cause a bit of a stir. Their names were Betty and Dolly and as my elder sister was already working, she used to take them to the local dances etc.

Our house used to be filled to overflowing at weekends with visitors, evacuees and family, including cousins and friends. There would be three or four to a double bed, most of us were girls, then there would be campbeds, people on the settee, in the bath, with of course a shake-up flock bed in it, and even on the floor. No-one was ever turned away from our house and we would all make the best of things for a night. Visitors would bring their little ration cards and all the points would be added up so that mother could obtain corned beef and other rationed items and with the eggs from our banties, potatoes, raspberries, peas, beans, cabbage etc from the garden, everyone would be well fed. Perhaps not the most spectacular of menus, but good, wholesome food served up in great quantities. One of mother's specialities was egg custard. Not just a little one, but it would be made in the largest meat tin and was enjoyed by many people during the war, including several airmen who used to visit from Desford Aerodrome where they were training and where my eldest sister worked on maintaining the planes.

Later on in the war we also had some more evacuees, after the others had left us, and these were a mother and daughter, Violet and Doreen Side, and they came to stay with us because Violet's husband was a fireman and as his brother Harry already lived in Ibstock, but did not have room for them, they moved in with us. This would be in 1943/44, as while they were with us I attended Coalville Grammar School and would be in my bedroom, and Doreen would be in hers playing schools by herself, but her talking to her pupils used to send me up the wall. Doreen and her mother were both fat, in fact Aunt Vi took a size 13 in mens' shoes, so you can imagine her girth. Doreen was about eighteen months younger than myself, but we never really hit it off together.

One day I was out shopping with Aunt Vi and Doreen and as we passed Billy Baker's shop in Chapel Street, we saw what we believed to be bananas being delivered. So on the way back from High Street we called in but were told they did not have any. You could only obtain such things on green ration books, which were for small children, but this did not make any difference. Aunt Vi was from the east end of London and used to use some very unusual words and the air was pretty blue that day. She used to come out with expressions which left us speechless, but to her they were ordinary conversation. The two of them stayed several months and her husband visited a few times and I remember him as a very tall, slim man.

This takes me on to the other Side family who lived in part of a house at the top of Gladstone Street, but on Melbourne Road. A village family lived in part and they lived in the other side, but I cannot remember if they had to share some of the facilities. The father, as I mentioned before, was Harry and his wife's name was Rose and she used to sing in the Ace Concert Party with my father. They also had a son, Ronnie, about my age, a daughter Joyce, and I believe a younger daughter. Ronnie was quite a nice young lad with fair hair, and somewhere among our old photos I have one of him with his bike. The family stayed several years, but over the years we have all lost touch.

The Allen family, who I think came from Ipswich, lived on Crown Hill and they also, I believe, shared a house with another village family. There were several children but the one I remember best was Eileen. She was about two years younger than me but was very small for her age and never grew much, about 4' 6" at the most, but after she left school she used to bike to Leicester to work.

There was a family named Dade living at the end of New Road and Chapel Street, but the only name that comes to mind is Sylvia, who had long auburn hair and was a very good looking girl. Another sister was Sophie.

While I have been writing this and talking to some of my relatives, I have realised that my cousin is married to one of our early evacuees and he has been here so long that I had forgotten. His name is Cyril Clarke who came from the Birmingham area and lived with Mr and Mrs Jordan. Mr Jordan was one of the local plumbers, and Cyril stayed on with them, making his life in Ibstock and he attended Coalville Grammar School at the same time as myself.

This concludes my memories and I have taken great pleasure from recalling all these people who have, or still are, part of the life of Ibstock, and many of them have enhanced life there over the years, making their homes among us and becoming good and trusted friends of the village, both in business, church and chapel life and in the ordinary stream of living.

Ibstock Penistone Rovers Football Club 1959

Ibstock Penistone Rovers Football Club

Formed in Penistone Street, Ibstock in July 1924, as Ibstock Penistone Football Club with 'Rovers' being added at a later date. Playing friendly fixtures in their early years they entered serious competition towards the end of the decade. The Club entered the Coalville and District Amateur League and went from strength to strength, moving to the well appointed Hastings Arms' Ground in 1933.

The Club figured strongly in the Leicestershire Senior League and the Central Amateur League during the 1930s and 40s before rejoining the Leicestershire Senior League, where they enjoyed a lasting spell until 1983. Three years of the Central Midlands League followed before 'Penistone' folded in May 1986, due to financial pressures.

The Club's history of success and achievement can easily be identified: numerous league championships together with an enviable list of cup competition trophies - The Leicestershire Junior Cup, Leicestershire Senior Cup, Coalville Charity Cup, Rolleston Charity Cup, Bass Charity Vase, Loughborough Charity Cup, Enderby Charity Cup, Barwell Charity Cup, to name just a few.

It must also be noted that throughout the Club's sixty-two year history only three secretaries were at the reins. George Wright, Bill Hands and Walter Bains all received long service awards from the Leicestershire County Football Association, the latter holding the position for thirty-one years.

The Hastings' Ground also played a major part in the Club's history, staging numerous County F.A. matches at Senior, Junior and Schoolboy level. One of the biggest attendances at the ground was in May 1976 when the Hastings' Ground was chosen to stage the final of English Schools Football Association under 16 competition between Coalville Upper School and Easington from County Durham.

The local Coalville Charity Cup Final was played there until the Club's demise in 1986.

David Smith

I was born in Ibstock on 14 July 1949 at my Grandfather's house. This was situated in Central Avenue, overlooking the Ibstock Penistone Rovers' football ground.

My Grandfather used to tell me about the match between Ibstock Colliery football team and Leicester City, when Ibstock lost 22-0. This match took place on 5 January 1924 and his brother, my Uncle Ben, was in goal. He always referred to the moment in the match when the City centre forward, Heathcock, was running through to score his ninth goal. Uncle Ben stood with arm aloft and shouted, "Stop!" Everybody did and the crowd went silent. When asked by the referee what was wrong, he said, "If he kicks that ball in the net again, he can fetch it out himself as I'm fed up with doing it!"

My Father, Harry Smith, played for the Penistone Rovers' team for fifteen years, after the war. During that time he was the team's penalty taker. In an article in 1958, in the Sports Mercury, it told of his great record as a penalty taker. It reported that Dad had only missed once in all that time. Nobody kept a score but it was thought that he scored over fifty goals from the spot.

After leaving Ibstock he played for nearby Nailstone M.W. and he scored three goals in a Cup Final on the Hastings Arms' ground including the winning goal from the penalty spot. The match was played on Easter Monday in front of a 1,500 crowd, including myself.

My Dad was in the middle of a controversy in 1952, with the very last kick of the match against Symingtons in the semi-final of the Senior Cup. He scored a penalty which put Ibstock through to the final. The ball cracked against the stanchion at the back of the net and shot out. An after-match argument took place as the spectators behind the goal had to convince those at the side who thought it had hit the post.

The Dancing Years by E Wilson

Take one Church Hall, a hundred or more teenagers, an embryo band, plus the Reverend Newbery, founding father of Ibstock's famous 'Tanner Hops' and the scene is set for the mid-1930s where my generation learned the gentle art of Slow-Slow-Quick-Quick-Slow. Hip Hop and Rap had totally different connotations sixty years ago, and today's frenetic twitchings would have had no place in our little world.

The Tanner Hops era brought about the formation of two local dance bands - the Regent and George Ayriss' Rhythm. As these bands became more proficient, bookings came in from a fairly wide area. On Saturdays, when Ibstock had no dance on offer, the band bus would load up in the High Street - drum kit at the back, then the rest of the instruments, followed by the musicians and their local supporters; we headed off for pastures new, such as Loughborough Palais, St George's Hall, Hinckley, Ratby, Swad Rink, Snarestone, and so on.

The Tanner Hops started around 7.30 p.m., no admission after 9.30 p.m., with the Last Waltz around 11.00 p.m. On New Year's Eve the jollifications went on until 1.00 a.m., as did mid-week dances, when, I may add, it was a race after the strains of the Last Waltz had died away between the dancers and the Lonely Wagon, guaranteed to take the edge off One Enchanted Evening if the back door was not slammed before our street was 'done'.

Let no-one belittle our interest in ballroom dancing - it was affordable to all and, moreover, *fun*. Sadly, 3rd September 1939 put paid to all that, as one by one we went our separate ways for the 'duration'.

In the early years of World War Two, we were sometimes fortunate in meeting up with our erstwhile dancing partners/band members, when on leave, as the W.M.C. hosted dances now and then but, as a general rule, The Billet, a Forces newspaper produced monthly in Coalville, was the only regular source of information we had of our one time 'Gang'. Some of the bandsmen were able, I believe, to team up with other bands wherever they found themselves but for the rest of us it was the end of a small segment of Ibstock's social history.

One of the big social events of the year was the Shrove Tuesday Whist Drive and Dance where the older generation indulged in cut throat games of whist (and heaven help anyone who trumped their partner's ace!) while the younger fry danced the night away, fuelled by the traditional refreshments. Salmon sandwiches, trifle, even, on occasions, lemonade and tea, were the norm.

The next major event was the Easter Monday Dance, Lent being strictly observed in those days. The Church Hall, in our day, was transformed for special occasions, with the hanging of streamers and balloons, plus, of course, a liberal dousing of chalk on the bare boards to facilitate our steps - no sprung or parquet floors for us.

Before the arrival of regular dances in Ibstock an older generation had somewhat scandalised the village elders by patronising Sunday night dances organised by Father Degen, a Catholic priest in Coalville, but that is another story.

My Father, the Singing Miner by Iris Gleeson

When I was very small, my father, Fred Storer, worked for Balfour Beatty as a labourer digging the trenches for the electricity cables, as the electricity was being introduced to the area at that time. My father was part of a team carrying out the work, and they left home on a Monday morning, returning the following Saturday lunchtime. They were all too poor to be able to pay for accommodation, so the big wooden spools which held the cable, like a giant cotton reel, were used at the ends and tarpaulins were stretched over them to form a large tent-like area in which they slept and ate their meals, cooking over an open fire.

This work of course was very hard and his hobby was to sing. He never had a singing lesson in his life but sang ballad type songs, similar to the ones sung by Richard Tauber, such as The White Dove, my favourite Bless This House, The Holy City, Six Feet of Earth, and many others.

During his period of work in the Ansty, Shilton, Wolvey area, near to Coventry, he, along with his pals, went to a local Church Social and while he was there he gave them a song or two. The next day, a lady came along to their working area asking for the man who had sung, and father came to meet her.

The lady, I do not know her name unfortunately, was a local singing teacher and thought that my Dad had a lot of potential. Through her, my father went to Birmingham to another teacher for an audition, and after that the lady wanted him to take professional lessons and she would pay all his expenses, but because he had three young daughters at that time, I was the youngest, he would not take the chance, although the lady said that he would soon have been able to repay her. Life for the family could have been so changed, as at that time he was earning about 10d per hour and having to work all hours to make ends meet. Still we all had a good life with lots of love and that can be more important than money.

Father kept on with his singing until well after the war. In fact he kept singing until his breathing became too bad for him to carry on.

He was known as The Singing Miner because he changed his job about the time of the outset of World War Two, and went to work at Whitwick Colliery. Even as early as this Whitwick had pithead baths, therefore he was able to come home clean, instead of having to be scrubbed in front of the fire as many men were.

During the war my father belonged to several Concert Parties, but the main one was The Ace in which I joined him as a singer. The concert party was made up of singers, men, women and children, dancers, comedians, pianist, compere etc. All very amateur but putting in a lot of practice so that they gave a lot of enjoyment to many people. As you can appreciate, most of our work was done for charity, and we used to go along to hospitals such as Bretby Hall Orthopaedic, where there were many men who had been very badly wounded, and when they were a little better they were transferred to Thorpe Hall and Gopsal Hall and they would then be transported to Ibstock Working Men's Club, where we fed them and provided the entertainment for the evening.

Mother, Gertrude, at this time used to make most of the costumes which we all wore. The ladies were all dressed in red pleated skirts and white mandarin blouses, and the men had white trousers with red mandarin shirts, all made in satin. This was the uniform, but we all had others for our turn as our performance was called. My father sang at many functions and he sang for Leicestershire County Cricket Club on several occasions.

Father had several changes of jobs over the years. From mining he went to be a steward of Bardon Road Working Men's Club, and at this time the whole family were able to help him, as he had had several accidents at the colliery which made it almost impossible to do heavy work. He then became landlord of The Boot Inn at Ibstock, and in both of these he was ably supported by my dear mother. His last job was as a needle polisher for the Grieve Needle Co at Coalville, from which he retired at the age of 65.

Always a fine husband and father, he worked tirelessly for the good of his family. Not always well paid, but a man who made sure we were all well shod, well fed and had lots of love.

The 'Lawrence Block', Melbourne Road by F Wallace

Number seventy-four was built in the 1800s by my grandfather, Richard Lawrence. He kept a hardware shop and after he died in 1919 George Brown had it made into a butcher's shop. Number seventy-six - George Forman lived there, he sold and repaired shoes in a workshop in the back. Number seventy-eight - my brother, Harry Lawrence, lived there. He was Clerk to the Parish Council for many years. My grandfather built all three of these houses.

Number eighty was built by my father, Jabey Lawrence, in about 1905. I was born there and lived there until my mother died. We had a shop there selling toys and fancy goods, etc in the workshop at the back. My father had a studio upstairs and took photographs. Many Ibstock people will remember that. He used to frame pictures downstairs. Later on it was made into a printing works for many years.

My father served on the Parish Council for a time. I remember laying a brick with my name on it at the Wesleyan Reform stone-laying ceremony in 1911. I also remember going to Ibstock Council School in 1911.

Number eighty is now used by Elston's the plumbers. My husband and myself live at number seventy-eight.

Richard Lawrence in Melbourne Road

Reflections of 1926 as told to Paula Gretton

The miners' strike of 1926 must have hit the village hard. Most of the men would have been employed at one pit or another around the area. I can only write from information that was given to me by people who lived through it. I have an Aunt who was born at Burton-on-Trent, this was because my grandad, who was a striking miner, had gone to stay with relations and was working in the Bovril factory there. However, that didn't last long because as soon as they found out he was a miner out he went. Another relative, who was a child at the time, tells me the parish provided breakfast for the miners' children - porridge and tea one day, a slice of bread and margarine with the cup of cocoa another. She used to make her brother drink her cocoa because she hated it!

This story is true and told to me by one of my relations: 'A little bit of coal for the fire'.

It was for my mother, I wanted to do something for her. Oh, she was cheerful enough but when you caught her off guard she sometimes had such a desperate, haunted look on her face but who wouldn't be desperate in her position; a husband and grown-up sons on strike and six small mouths to feed. In fact she had ten mouths to feed altogether and the little ones were always hungry.

You see, she had no one to work with her, she was shouldering the burden all alone. My dad - all he was concerned about was number one!!

I sat on the door step thinking, I had to do something. The miners had been on strike for six months now and I thought surely this year - 1926 - will go down in history, with everyone having been on strike at one point in support of the miners. They said that London came to a complete standstill when the buses, trains and trams stopped running. What would I know about London? I'd never been there and I was never likely to, it could have been the moon as far as I was concerned.

It wasn't only wanting to help my mam made me want to do something, I was fed up. Being sixteen you were neither boy nor man and, day after day, the time hung heavy. Now that September had arrived, the nights were getting shorter and in the early morning and in the evening you could feel the autumn nip in the air. I'd asked mam yesterday if I should light a bit of fire, just to warm the house a bit before we went to bed but she wouldn't let me. There was hardly any coal in the coalhouse and what precious bit she did have she wanted to save for washday, so that she could get the copper boiling. My mam, you see, took in washing. Eight kids of her own and then she washed for someone else for half-a-crown!!

I walked up the fields trying to kill a bit of time, chewing a piece of hedge stalk to take away the hunger pains. The little ones needed what bit of food we'd got, I could get by. It was here I met Tommy Watkins and we cooked up our plan. Tommy told me that he'd heard that anyone who went back to work could fill a bag of coal from the slag heap. That was it, wouldn't my mam be pleased, we would, perhaps, then light a bit of fire in the evenings. We wouldn't really be breaking the strike, we wouldn't make much difference because we wouldn't be allowed down the pit, so we wouldn't actually be mining the coal only doing a few jobs on the pit top.

When the shift was finished I made my way to the heap. There was some good quality coal, it had just been dumped there, just to get it out of the way and I filled my sack. Like anything you get for free you tend to be a bit greedy and after carrying this sack for about a hundred yards I knew I was beat. Two miles I had to go, so I took some coal out and hid it under the hedge. I would go back for it tomorrow. I was determined to get this bag of coal home even if it meant stopping and resting every few yards. What an object I must have looked, black as the coal I was carrying. My back felt like it was breaking in two and my shoulders were on fire, but I had to do it. It was the look on my mam's face that kept me going.

I walked down the bridle, it took for ages but soon my journey was near its end. Coming past the cemetery into Curzon Street I thought I could hear something. Straining to listen I could hear a band. No, it was not possible, carrying this load must have been giving me hallucinations. But no, I could distinctly hear a band playing and the noise was getting closer and closer.

When I saw what it was, my heart came into my mouth and then sank deep into my stomach. I felt sick. Coming along High Street was a procession of men, striking miners marching behind the band, and what was even worse, there in the front carrying the miners' union flag was my dad!! What could I do? If ever they saw me, that would be the end of me, they'd skin me alive. They weren't very sympathetic to blacklegs and my dad would be so angry to be shown up in front of his friends. I dodged into somebody's entry, praying they wouldn't come out of the house and find me, I pressed myself hard against the wall so no-one walking by would see me.

The procession stopped at the corner of Chapel Street and I cautiously peeped around the corner of the wall. A very distinguished looking gentleman with a big moustache climbed onto a beer crate to speak to the crowd. He was such an eloquent speaker, one of those sort that could really get a crowd going. He had that sort of voice that could persuade you to do anything. He talked about the poor working man breaking his back to feather the pockets of the rich and how the Tories didn't care tuppence about them. The crowd cheered his every shout. "Will we be defeated?" he cried. "No, never!" shouted the men. "What shall we do with the blacklegs?" he asked. "Hunt them out and teach them a lesson they'll never forget!" shouted someone from the crowd. "Will we go back to work?" he then asked. The crowd were in uproar. "Never! Never! Never!"

With each crowd response, my dad waved this flag like a madman. The more the crowd shouted and cheered, the more he waved the flag, getting up on a crate himself so that all the crowd could see him. My legs were all of a tremble. I thought

I was going to faint. Would they come up this street past where I was trying to hide. Someone somewhere must have been watching over me for they turned left and marched off up Chapel Street, no doubt to stand and sing and shout up by the Hastings Arms.

When I was quite sure they had gone, I crept out, slung the sack over my shoulders, and made for home as fast as my legs would carry me and this load of coal would allow. The look of surprise and delight I received from my mam was worth everything; the effort, the hard work and the fright I had endured.

"Sammy, are you ready for your dinner, lad?" my mam asked softly. "Not just yet mam. I'll just have five minutes shuteye," I replied. She covered the settee with a piece of clean sacking and I just fell onto it and was asleep in two seconds.

To this day my dad doesn't know about his blackleg son nearly being caught out by him and his merry band.

Mary Jane Preston and Dolly Sperry (tape-recording)

I can remember the 1926 strike. My father was one of those miners on strike. Times were very hard for the family.

We can remember our first day at school. We held hands because we were scared stiff of the boys. They didn't put us in age groups then. I went home one day and told my mam that I'd passed our Harry in my school work. And she said, "Ah, well, our Harry's been poorly." He was about three years older than me. We learnt all sorts at school but the worst lesson we had was sewing. It was awful and I was no good at it. We didn't make anything, we just used bits of rag to sew. We went to the Church of England school and we learned about the Bible mostly. We played games like tig, kiss in the ring and we played rounders.

There used to be an old man, Georgie Cornwall, who kept a shop and as children we daren't go in there. It was alright if you were grown up but we daren't. They'd send you in for a pennyworth of something and you'd get it and run out quick.

We used to have sixpence a week pocket money. Tuppence to go to the Palace on Saturday morning and a ha'pennyworth of sweets, if you were lucky. They were silent pictures and a lady played the piano. At the end of the serial, Pearl White was always tied to the railway lines and I thought she had to lie there tied to the lines until the next week.

I could have gone to the Grammar School but my mam couldn't afford to let me go. I had to stop at home and help my mam. I'd got three brothers and two sisters; I was the eldest girl so I had to help her with the children. A lady came and asked me to go and look after her children. My mam said she didn't want me to be a skivvy. She said she'd been a skivvy and didn't want me to. But I did go and earned enough to buy the bread and the milk for our family. The lady was Mrs Mears and she lived at the farmhouse. She'd got two children and I used to watch them for her. The family went to Australia and Mr Mears' mam who was an old lady asked me to go and do her washing for her but my mam said again that I wasn't to be a skivvy so I went to work in a shoe factory in Earl Shilton.

We used to meet boys by walking round the streets and then we'd go walking with them. If you had some money you went to the pictures. If you hadn't you went down Overton Road - it was called Locker's Lane then. We never dared do anything wrong. Our mothers used to say, "If you get into trouble, you'll go to the workhouse." It frightened us to death. I used to visit a friend's mother in the workhouse and it was terrible. It was clean but when you've said that you've said everything. It was really grim. I believe they found a new born baby in a tin trunk, years ago in the spinney opposite Dr Cantrell's. They never found out whose it was.

I was twenty-eight when I got married because we were waiting for a house. We couldn't afford to buy one. We were lucky, we managed to rent a cottage at the side of Gladstone Street. There was a kitchen, a sitting room and two bedrooms and the toilet was up the garden. We didn't have enough ground for a garden but we had an allotment near to the Junior School. That was my husband's hobby and it kept us in vegetables. He loved his allotment.

Dorothy Bott (tape-recording)

When I was a child, I had to stay at home because my mother was so ill. I only went to school for the odd day. I was told I had to go to see the Attendance Officer. I had to take my baby sister with me and I was terrified that I was going to be told off. In the school, my sister, who was just beginning to talk, saw a picture of some ducks coming, dirty, from out of a tunnel. She said, "Ooh. Look at dat dere mucky duck." The man asked me why I hadn't been to school but he knew the reason and was just trying me out. I had to say that it was because of my mother being so ill and there were seven of us in the family. The Attendance Officer said, "Dorothy, I've come to tell you that you needn't come to school any more." I never went to school after the age of nine.

When I got older, an uncle came to tell my mother that he wanted to help her by taking one of us. He said he would take me because he thought I was the most capable. When I went to live with him at Woodville, I hadn't got a room to sleep in. I slept on the landing in the space where the stairs came up. He kept a lot of dogs and if I hadn't cleaned them out to his satisfaction, he used to get the dirty mop and rub it in my face. I got so tired and fed up that I ran away.

My friend tried to get me a job in service. She went to London as a nursemaid and I could have gone too but I couldn't as I had nothing to go with. I did get a nice place, eventually, and for a time I worked for Dr Meldrum and Dr Watts, mainly doing cooking.

Just before the war, my husband and I took a small-holding at Osbaston. We kept poultry although all we knew about it was from keeping hens at home, but we did it. We had pigs and a thousand head of poultry when the war broke out. I have helped to kill a pig and have made pork pies and all sorts of things.

Memory told to Paula Gretton

As I stand and watch the traffic hurtling down Melbourne Road I think back to my childhood. Seventy years ago it was a rare sight to see a motorised vehicle so we as kids had a freedom that the children of today will never know.

We could play in the road, sit on the kerb playing marbles and snobs. Although playing football was an offence we all did it but a glimpse of the policeman on his bike would send kids scattering in all directions. We did think ourselves lucky if we could persuade Mr Ottey to give us a bit of orange box string to use as a skipping rope and we were even more delighted if Mam's washing line broke so we could use that. We played all sorts of running, chasing and circle games like tin-a-lurkey. These games we would make up for ourselves as we had none of the expensive toys kids have nowadays.

If it was wet we would play in the wash house. All the kids from the row would crowd in and we would have a show or a play that we made up ourselves. The only problem on our yard was Norman Dolman, he always had to be ghost just because his mother had a pair of white gloves. We all in turn entreated, "Norman, let me borrow the gloves to be the ghost." "No, my mam will kill me if I lose them". So the ghost part always went to him.

What simple pleasures entertained us as kids!

Are You Going out Tonight? told to Paula Gretton

When I was a child seventy years ago this statement didn't mean you were off out to have a good time, to the pub or dancing perhaps. It meant the men were off out poaching. There used to be a famous poacher who lived down the yard near the Melbourne Road off licence and early Saturday evening my mother used to send me down to ask his wife Eliza if he was going out that night. I hated going because she was quite a formidable figure and as I knocked at the door I would be trembling. You know the feeling "frit to death and done nowt". "Yes, my girl," she'd say. "Tell your mam he'll be across with one in the morning".

I was then sent to Jake Fletcher's butcher's shop for sixpenny worth of shin. This was going to be our Sunday lunch. The shin of beef and all the vegetables were put in the brown stew pot in the coal oven early on Sunday morning. The rabbit would have appeared on the back doorstep and had to be cleaned and gutted before being added to the stew for the last half an hour. It didn't take much cooking and the meat was lovely and tender.

A friend of mine when she was still a child used to have to go round and ask various villagers if they wanted a rabbit. Her brother was quite a dab hand at catching them. She had to take them round the next day. Once she went to one old lady's house and presented her with her ninepenny rabbit. " Oh, no my dear," the old lady said, "I ordered a shilling one." Back she went home and said to her brother, "Old lady .... says she ordered a shilling rabbit." "Give it here," said her brother and did no more than tie the rabbit's legs to the pump handle and then pull the handle up so the rabbit stretched. "Here, take this one and tell her it's her shilling rabbit."

Pinkie Bartlett

We came to Ibstock in 1966 - nearly thirty years ago - it seems a long time now when I think of the changes in the village since then. When I came here I was fairly new to England (having been born in Sri Lanka). Despite my early trepidations, I found the people so charming and, as they all seemed to know each other, I soon found that I was accepted into the village. It took me some time to remember their names then. Now that we have the 'new estates' so many of the people that I meet in High Street are virtually strangers.

In the '60s, High Street appeared to have more life than now. Over those thirty years the cinema has closed plus one of the petrol stations, a bank, a sub-post office and quite a few of the old shops. Yet the population of the village has increased.

101

Behind our house we had open fields in the '60s - the children were younger then and they were happy to be able to play with home-made boomerangs where there are now hundreds of new houses and gardens. It seems that their occupants must all shop at the new supermarkets outside the village.

Soon after arriving in the village, I found myself running the Brownies and Girl Guides, and, later, getting involved with the Church Council and the Parish Council. It was one way of getting to know people. Those organisations still exist supported, mainly, by the 'old inhabitants' of the village.

My Memories of Ibstock by Vivien Parry

I was born on the 23 March 1948 in Alperton, Wembley, Middlesex, in a terraced house. The house had bay windows in the front room and front bedroom. The house comprised the following rooms: two reception rooms, three bedrooms, kitchen, bathroom and separate toilet.

In 1966, whilst on holiday in Italy, I met my future husband, who lived in Ellistown. Eventually, we married in 1969 and went to live on High Street, Ibstock. That's when I realised that things I had taken for normal were now in the past. We moved into two rooms with a conservatory on the back, no bathroom and a toilet down the garden, about 20 yards from the conservatory door. This distance seemed like miles in the middle of the night! When we first moved in the toilet didn't have any light in it so my husband and my dad put this in; the light was switched on and off in the conservatory. The toilet had a tiled roof - just the sort of place that spiders love to live, but thankfully this was boarded in later.

I think in the three years that we lived in Ibstock I regularly had to walk down the garden in the middle of the night to use the toilet. Rainy weather was the worst, especially in the cold of winter, as I would have to stop and put on my boots and thick coat and find an umbrella. After a while I learnt to keep the umbrella by the door for these night time adventures.

I remember, one evening we had been watching The Pit and the Pendulum, a horror film. After it had finished I had to visit the toilet. It was very windy that evening and the wind was whistling through the trees outside and the branches were tapping on the toilet roof. I was sitting there, as you do, when the light went out. I remember thinking that I'd sit there all night rather than go out in the dark. I'm not usually frightened of the dark but at the end of the horror film the heroine is left to rot in a dark dungeon. After about three or four minutes the light came on again and I ran back indoors. My husband had switched the light off for a laugh - he thought it might scare me. He was right, it did.

Having always lived in houses with a bathroom it was really strange not to have one. As my husband worked as a maintenance engineer for the colliery, he had a shower daily before he left work. Unfortunately, I wasn't so lucky, I had to rely on friends. One friend offered me the use of her bath and supplied towel, soap and even bubble-bath, in fact, the works. Another friend said any time I wanted a bath just to ask, so I did. This friend supplied just the bath water, nothing else. Luckily I'd taken soap and a towel with me - otherwise I'd have been in a bit of a mess. It just shows that 'a bath' means different things to different people.

Having lived on the outskirts of London until I was fourteen I was used to London fogs - but not indoors!! As my husband worked for the colliery he received a concessionary coal allowance. We had one fire place which was fine until the wind changed direction, then the smoke came down the chimney and filled the room. It was terrible! Various contraptions were fitted to the chimney but to no avail, in fact, it got worse.

Whilst living in Ibstock we had a dog and, I must admit, there were some lovely walks in the fields behind our accommodation. If the cows were grazing in the fields when we took the dog down there she would run away as fast the wind, as she was terrified of them.

After three years of living in Ibstock we moved to a new house in Ashby-de-la-Zouch, thankfully, with a bathroom and inside toilet!!

Minutes of an early meeting of the Council or Witan of Ibba's Stock - 10th July 789 Anno Domini

Apologies were received from Hrothgar and Jan Bloodysword who were out pillaging along the Mease.

The Chairman, Ibba, smashed a hand's breadth of good oak from the end of the table with his battleaxe and called for order.

Item one: Cattle stealing. Sweyne Halfshank said he thought it was a good idea. The Chairman hurled a drinking horn at him and explained that it was the stealing of Ibba's cattle that was the problem. After discussion is was agreed to raise the Byelaw penalty from Death to Transportation to Norway.

Item two: Complaints had been received about the level of fighting and rioting in the streets. The Chairman said he was very disappointed that only four fights had been reported in June. Norbert Bearsark added that the one involving Sweyne Halfshank didn't really count as it was like watching a little girl play with her kitten. Sweyne replied that at least his wife was not available for passing Saxons at a discount price. The meeting was interrupted for a few moments while Norbert clove Sweyne in two from skull to navel. The Chairman said he found this most encouraging.

Item three: The clerk, Father Bedwyr, reported that the War Boat building project had so far cost three hundred gold pieces and that he was wondering how it was going to be launched as the village was over fifteen leagues from the sea. The Council unanimously agreed that this was typical of a weak-kneed, pacifist priest and they were sure that it would be a useful facility for the whole village.

Item four: The Temple of Odin Lads and Girls had applied for a grant for their summer Rampage. Last year's had been a great success with fourteen dead and over twenty wounded. The Council agreed to raze a nearby Saxon settlement to the ground and donate the proceeds to the Rampage.

Item five: It was reported that Lars Cnut had dug up some black rocks in his field and was burning them as fuel. The Council agreed that this would never catch on. And anyway what was wrong with burning trees, houses, witches, boats and churches?

At this point Karl Sigurson made an off-colour remark about Cnut's name and was dealt with by the Chairman. After the body was removed the Council proceeded to....

Item six: Jehan Kaleflower, the potter, suggested filling the valley at the bottom of the village with fourteen thousand cartloads of cowdung. The Council suggested that this was a lot of shite ... Jehan agreed and asked if thirteen cartloads would be any better? The Council explained that he had misunderstood them and that doing so could be fatal.

Item seven: Pinkeye Bjornson suggested that the village could be improved by hanging skulls from the houses and lantern posts to warn and frighten visitors. An amendment was moved by Odo Mailfist that it would be nice if they were hollowed out and filled with flowers. The Chairman remarked that he had always suspected that there was something wrong with Odo and that he would personally slaughter the first person who put flowers in the village. The original motion was carried unanimously after the Chairman had given Odo a hard stare.

There being no further items the Council shouted "Wass Hail", filled flowing horn from fine-frothing firkin and drank themselves into unconsciousness.

A Walk Down Locker's Lane by Audrey Kendrick

I leave the busy road behind
And sense my mind at ease,
Then forward past the Manor
To the arch of leaf-decked trees.

A soft breeze breaks the silence
The air is scented sweet,
From woodbine, wild upon the briar
Yet not a soul to greet.

Light steps will take me onward
To the gate where cattle stand,
Patient, waiting for the call
Of the farmer's hired hand.

I see the cottage on the hill
That watched the centuries unfold,
And over the hill the road runs down
To stop at the brook on the road.

My memory recalls the old duck pond
And the farm house side by side,
The hay cart toting heavy loads
On roads a mere six foot wide.

I hear the skylark, now I pause
To savour the sweetest refrain,
And now I know why in days gone by
Folk called this old road Lover's Lane.

bstock Church Avenue

Other local books available from Coalville Publishing include:

Cinema in Coalville

Hugglescote

Getting the Coal

One Man's Moira

and the best selling Loose Poetry

Forthcoming title:

Coalville Publishing Company is planning to commemorate the opening of the Ivanhoe Line, which is a new passenger train service for Leicestershire and South Derbyshire. The service will be fully operational in 1995 with 16 new stations providing an hourly service from Loughborough to Leicester on via Coalville and Burton-on-Trent to Derby. A unique collection of photographs and reminiscences of the line, dating from the age of steam will be published to coincide with this event. You can obtain a copy of this book, at a reduced price, by subscribing in advance.

Details of all the above and all other publications from:

Coalville Publishing Co Ltd

The Springboard Centre

Mantle Lane

Coalville

Leicestershire

LE67 3DW

Telephone: Coalville (0530) 839531